Make Me a Match

Make Me a Match

The Complete Guide to Using a
Modern Matchmaker to Find True Love

Matchmaking Institute^{SM}
Introduction by Lisa Clampitt, CSW

Skyhorse Publishing

Skyhorse Publishing books may be purchased in bulk at special discounts for sales promotion, corporate gifts, fund-raising, or educational purposes. Special editions can also be created to specifications. For details, contact the Special Sales Department, Skyhorse Publishing, 307 West 36th Street, 11th Floor, New York, NY 10018 or info@skyhorsepublishing.com.

Skyhorse® and Skyhorse Publishing® are registered trademarks of Skyhorse Publishing, Inc.®, a Delaware corporation.

Visit our website at www.skyhorsepublishing.com

10 9 8 7 6 5 4 3 2 1

Library of Congress Cataloging-in-Publication Data is available on file.

ISBN: 978-1-61608-690-9

Interior design by Elise Smith

Printed in the United States of America

Table of Contents

PART III   *Additional Materials*

Introduction

by Lisa Clampitt, CSW

I am a true romantic. I believe that people operate at their all-time best if they have a happy, healthy, supportive, and respectful partner in their life. It's a commonly known fact that people are more productive at work, healthier both physically and emotionally, live longer, and thrive in all areas of their life if they are involved in a mutually loving, enriching relationship.

In today's fast paced life, we engage experts to help us be the best we can be in all areas of life. We hire an accountant to complete our tax forms because most of us don't know every tax deduction or new tax law that is beneficial to our unique situation. We hire a real estate agent to help us find a home that fits our exact requirements. How else would we know what houses are available? We even hire a personal trainer to keep our weight goals on track and our body in shape. Of course, we go to doctors for checkups to keep our bodies healthy. Yet we tend to feel reluctant about seeking help when it comes to life's most complicated and pleasurable aspect—our love life.

Our personal love life tends to be the most neglected area and yet the most important in terms of overall happiness. I have witnessed great sadness and isolation in people who feel they just can't find someone who is right for them. They have tried looking in bars, going to parties and even searching online to meet that special someone . . . with absolutely no luck. I have seen people lose hope, convinced they will never find or experience the love of a lifetime that they so desire.

As a professional matchmaker, I am here to tell you that I have seen and helped people who felt love is impossible for them find the impossible. Love does have the power to transform your life. I have seen it happen time and time again. And it is available to everyone!

I wrote this book to assure people they can absolutely find love. *Make Me a Match* answers such questions as: Why am I single? What do I need to do to find that special person? What is a matchmaker? Why should I use one? What can I expect throughout the process? How do I find love? Will I be successful?

"Matchmakers truly believe in their ability to help people find love."

I have dedicated my life to making people's dreams of finding true love become a reality. It isn't magic—it takes insight and deep understanding of yourself and the choices you make each step of the way. Nobody teaches us how to do this. Yet we somehow believe we should be our own expert in the romantic arena and feel ashamed if we fail. So it's no surprise that we flounder in our search for love. With a qualified professional at your side to offer you insight, honesty, and constructive feedback, you can gain insight into yourself and your partner choices and actually start on your path to finally being successful in not only finding your true love but making sure it is one that will last a lifetime.

PART I

Matchmaking: Making a Perfect Match

Why Haven't I Found Mr. or Mrs. Right?

1

You want love in your life and haven't found "the one." It is my firm belief that no one should be without a partner if they truly want one. So, let's explore your current life situation and determine the best way to go about finding Mr. or Mrs. Right.

You Have Never Married.

Today, there are more single people living by themselves than ever before. In fact, marriage rates in the United States are at historic lows. Why? Because people are living longer, birth control is widespread, and women are pursuing career paths that make them financially secure. And with people living well into their eighties, it makes sense to approach marriage cautiously. After all, settling down in your mid twenties means spending six decades with the same person—making it more important than ever to find a partner who truly shares your values, morals, and life goals. I strongly recommend taking whatever time is necessary to choose a partner wisely. But I also urge you to take an honest look at what obstacles may be getting in the way of you finding the right person.

Do You Have Unrealistic Expectations?

Are you—a quiet, shy, average looking, forty-year-old librarian—looking for a tall, dark, handsome thirty-year-old investment banker? Or do you—an overweight fifty-five-year-old plumber—only want to date slender, twenty-two-year-old bombshells? If so, you are really limiting your options. Nicole Leclerc, a matchmaker and owner of Compatibles in Vermont finds that her male clients tend to start out with completely unrealistic expectations. "Paul sent me his list of criteria for women he wanted to be introduced to. I always appreciate this, as it's a great place to start the relationship with a new client. But I couldn't help thinking that the list of criteria Paul sent was a joke. Turns out he was one hundred percent serious. He had listed women's bra cup sizes that were acceptable to him, women's shoe sizes, measurements of hips, thighs, calves, ankles, and waist all to the inch! I was stunned and told him I could not offer the degree of scrutiny he wanted for these physical attributes—I do not measure my clients or ask their bra cup size. However, I do have wonderful women that I was certain he'd find attractive if he could be a little more flexible." Wonderful human beings are packaged in all sorts of unique ways. Be adventurous and consider opening up to more possibilities.

Are You a Workaholic?

Do you spend more time and energy on your work than on your personal life? If you're consumed by your job, it's time to take a look at why. What are you avoiding? Why are you letting work dominate your life? Julie Ferman a matchmaker in Oak Park, California talks about her client Darryl, a thirty-eight-year-old management consultant who spends twenty days a month on the road building his own management consulting business and living the life of a workaholic. In time, he plans to hire enough junior consultants to take over the long-distance travel gigs because also high on his list of life goals is marriage and family. His current problem is finding and lining up first dates with women who may be "marriage material" for him. "He hired me to be his 'love broker,' to sift and sort and line up the most fitting candidates for him to meet on the ten or so days a month he's home in Los Angeles. The plan—by the time his business is developed he'll be engaged or married, and by the time the kids are born, well, he'll be traveling much less and able to be a family man. Darryl and I keep in touch via e-mails and voice mail messages and through monthly telephone coaching calls, and he's enjoying the process of meeting what he considers to be qualified candidates. He's learning how to date, how to relate with women at a higher level and he calls this process one of 'grooming him to be a groom.'" After all, nobody's dying wish is that they had spent more time at the office.

Do You Tend to Make Unwise Partner Choices?

Are you attracted to the bad boy types? You know, the tall, dark, mysterious, larger-than-life guys who are all over you one minute and seem to just disappear the next? Or do the wild party girls, blonde, bubbly, and fun excite you most? Anne Teachworth, certified Matchmaker and author of *Why We Pick the Mates We Do* says, "It has been my experience, taking family of origin histories, that women who like 'bad boys' and men who like 'wild girls' consistently had a parent who was a 'bad boy or girl.' Their 'chemistry' attraction to that type is programmed in at an unconscious level and they need the direction of a good matchmaker to intervene and effect a change in their mating pattern."

Are You Socially Awkward or Shy?

Many people aren't comfortable in social situations. If you are a little awkward socially or just plain shy, you probably prefer solitary activities like reading, watching television, and surfing the web. That's fine, but it's important to get out. The only way to become more comfortable is to throw yourself into social situations as often as possible and, as the saying goes, "fake it until you make it." The more you get out and interact, the more comfortable you'll feel. But it is hard for us to break our life-long patterns. Going from social isolation to social butterfly can be extremely difficult. In fact, we often make excuses to avoid the discomfort of change in an attempt to keep our status quo at all costs. Rob Anderson of Club Elite, a matchmaking service in New York City for gay men, tells a story of his client Jeff, who had a tendency toward nesting and isolating himself in his apartment. "When Jeff called asking about our Club Elite service, we talked about what he was looking for in a mate, and after a lengthy discussion, he said, 'To be honest—I just moved into a new apartment and I'm torn between spending the money on your service or the new couch I have been eyeballing and really want.' I didn't hear back from him so I guessed he opted for the couch. Six months later—out of the blue—Jeff called again. 'Did you get that couch you were in love with?' I asked. 'Yes,' he replied, 'and I'm sitting on it all alone.' He joined Club Elite and after a few dates met someone he is extremely happy with. He is so grateful and I love the vision I have of them cuddling on that couch."

Do You Have Limited Access to Potential Partners?

If all your friends are married or coupled, if you don't date work colleagues or work from home, if you belong to a same sex gym, and if you haven't found time to volunteer in your community or join social organizations, then finding potential partners may be difficult. And remember, the older we get the further we are from our school days where single classmates were in abundance and our exposure to potential mates was great. So now you need to be more proactive in order to gain access to wonderful single people who may be compatible mates. You need to branch out. Ask everyone you know if they have a friend who may enjoy going out with you. Make a list of all your family members and friends. As you write these names down, old friends you haven't seen lately will come to mind. Invite them out for a drink and ask if they have a single friend they can introduce you to. There really is no down side to asking. They may not be able to come up with a prospect right there on the spot. But in a week or two, they just might call back having remembered a single friend who's perfect for you.

I had a friend from graduate school who still lived in the Midwest and didn't have a lot of access to single people because she worked long hours. I gave her my advice about asking everyone she knew to think of someone for her. So she called one of her old friends that she had not talked to in a while and asked him if he knew any men to introduce her to. At first he couldn't think of anyone, and he too was working crazy hours. But my friend didn't let him off the hook. She kept calling and one night took him out for dinner. Over dinner, the more they talked and she described what she was looking for, he then remembered an old high school friend of his who had just finished his law degree and was single. He introduced them and they dated for over a year. He didn't end up being the love of her life, but he remains a great friend to this day. You never know who people will think of when given a little push.

Do You Choose Unavailable Partners?

Are you attracted to emotionally distant, unavailable types? Is the love of your life married? Or is he constantly on the road traveling? "My client Rachel's last two boyfriends lived out of state," relates Anne Teachworth of Perfect Mate in New Orleans. "She came to our matchmaking office in desperation wanting to know why this always happens to her. She wanted someone to go to parties with, not airports, and wondered if I could find someone for her who lived locally. She worked as a medical drug sales representative traveling in the southeast region. Traveling was familiar for her—so was loneliness. Her childhood history revealed her attraction pattern. She grew up on military bases, the child of an air force captain, and constantly moved from base to base. Rachel, like the other army kids, was always leaving classmates and moving to new schools—good-bye was such a familiar scene that she hardly minded it. Based on this history, I knew Rachel needed someone who would not be leaving town or someone who could take her with him. Jim was perfect. A salesman, he worked the same southeast region her company covered. He had been looking for a gal who could get used to his traveling. His last girlfriend constantly complained that he wasn't available. Rachel was much like Jim . . . They met and have been happy on the road together ever since. In fact, they have coordinated their sales calls so they travel to the same towns at the same times. They are so happy together and yet they never would have met had they not worked with a matchmaker who understood who they are and exactly what they are looking for in a mate."

5

Are You Viewing Partners Through Marriage Eyes?

If you are in your thirties, chances are you're wondering if each potential partner is marriage material. Rather than causally going out, having fun, exploring the person's uniqueness, you are looking at them and wondering if this person could be the parent of your children, the "one" you will spend the rest of your life with. You're probably asking yourself, "Can I actually make my life with this person?" instead of just enjoying each moment of getting to know one another. Approaching any budding relationship with marriage eyes puts too much pressure on the relationship too quickly. Give yourself time to discover, explore, and play with each new partner.

I once worked with a woman who was thirty five years old and in a hurry to get married and have kids. She tried to go on as many dates as possible to sift through "who was serious and who was wasting her time." Any potential great guys were scared off by her Spanish Inquisition–style— they wanted to get to know her and instead were being interviewed and questioned ad nauseum. By looking at each date through marriage eyes, I believe she sabotaged her own time frame and made the process of finding "the one" much more difficult. If she had relaxed and gotten to know her dates, and let her dates get to know her, they may have been able to see what a wonderful woman she was and enjoyed getting to know her.

Newly Divorced or Separated

You miss the companionship of the opposite sex, want to start dating, and don't know where to start. Rest assured you are not alone. Dating after divorce can feel daunting. But it doesn't have to. I urge you to take it slowly and have fun. Remember you are an attractive, interesting person who deserves to go out and enjoy yourself. Approach dating with an explorer's sense of adventure!

One of my clients was very nervous when he got divorced. He was used to having someone in his life on a daily basis and didn't know if he had the knack for small talk. After the first few dates with a couple different women, he found that he loved getting to know new people and actually saw a curious and social side to himself that he forgot he had. Dating again after a divorce can be a wonderful time for relearning about yourself as a social creature. Take advantage of this time and have fun.

Feeling Anxious and Out of the Dating Loop?

It's natural to feel a bit disoriented and insecure as you try to navigate dating after having settled down for what you thought was "until death do us part." Give yourself a break and remember that you're a beginner again. Approach it as you would any new activity. Your date is probably nervous too, so try to relax, be yourself, smile, and before you know it, you'll both be more at ease. Dating is about getting to know another person and seeing if you enjoy their company. If the first few dates don't go as you hoped, take note of what worked and what didn't and view it as a learning opportunity.

One of my clients tended to talk too much on dates because he was nervous. He felt if he opened up and told them all about himself, his dates would be impressed and like him even more. This in fact was not the case. People like it when you are curious about them and ask questions to balance the conversation. His dates thought he was too self-involved and lost interest pretty quickly. This, of course, was the opposite of his intention.

Is Your Dating Mode Outdated?

Are you hitting the bar scene the way you did before you got married? Or going to the same places you did with your ex? Dating strategies and venues that worked when you were a young single or comfortable married may not be right for you in this new life stage.

I had a client that would take his dates to the same place he used to go with his ex because he felt comfortable and knew the staff there. The only problem was that everyone there knew him when he was married and would talk about the past with him. This made his dates feel uncomfortable and left out. Avoid trying to recreate the past. Instead, get involved in new activities and find new places to go that intrigue you. If you meet an interesting member of the opposite sex, say at a book signing, don't expect sparks to fly immediately. Get to know this individual—talk about commonalities, take a walk together. As you begin to feel comfortable with this person, you may be surprised at how romantic feelings just naturally develop. Be open to new ways of approaching dating.

Think About Different Partner Choices

Divorce provides a unique opportunity for personal growth. It gives you the time and wherewithal to focus on yourself and examine your values, life goals, and interests separate and apart from your ex. Keep in mind that what you wanted at age twenty-five may not be what's important to you at age forty. If you take the time to learn who you are and what qualities are important to you now, you're assured of making more satisfying, empowering partner choices. One of my clients was thrilled to discover that he was a lot more adventurous now that his kids were grown. He realized that he wanted to meet a woman he could travel the world and explore with rather than someone that would help him raise his kids. He loved being able to share common interests with his dates that he had not thought about since he was in his twenties.

Widowed

Dating after a spouse dies is especially difficult because the loss is involuntary and unexpected. Memories of wonderful times spent together make it difficult to imagine getting involved with someone new. Certainly losing the love of your life is painful, yet being alone for the rest of your life is also painful.

Comparing Potential Partners to Your Deceased Spouse

It's hard not to compare new partners to your deceased spouse, and yet it sets each date up for disaster. You can't have the shared history, commitment, and years of devotion with someone new that you enjoyed with your spouse. So stop comparing your date to your spouse—no one will measure up. Instead, notice the special qualities this new person has to offer. Acknowledge and honor the newness. Allow yourself to fully experience the uniqueness another individual can bring to your life.

One of my clients kept telling me that each of the dates I introduced him to were not as smart, attractive, or funny as his deceased wife. Until one day, I introduced him to someone who was an avid skier. His wife hadn't skied and he forgot how much he loved going to the mountains on the weekend to ski. Once he and this new woman started skiing together, he began to open up, enjoyed discovering this woman's depth of character and decided to give it a chance—to get to know someone else and her uniqueness.

Feelings of Betrayal
On the one hand you may feel like you're betraying your deceased spouse by having feelings for another and on the other hand you may feel like you're betraying your new partner by still loving your spouse. Dealing with these feelings of guilt and betrayal is a part of the experience of being a healthy, active, dating widow. Of course nobody can replace your deceased spouse, but if you meet someone whose company you enjoy, think of this person as someone who may want to share the next chapter in your life's adventure with you.

One of my clients had a wonderful relationship with his wife, who died after a long bout with cancer. They were able to discuss what life would be like after her death, and she wanted him to find another love so that he would not be alone. This was very hard for him to accept at first. However, over time he realized that he too would have wanted the same for her and he owed it to himself to honor life by continuing to live.

Letting Go and Creating a New Life

As happy as you and your spouse were together, and as terrible as becoming a widow feels, you will continue to live. More than anything, you need to give yourself permission to experience joy, both alone and with others. Julie Ferman's client Neil came to see her a couple of years after losing his wife of thirty years to breast cancer. The post-date feedback on Neil kept coming back with the same criticism—Neil talks about his wife all the time. If, for example, travel was the topic of conversation, he would speak about the trip he and Nancy had taken to Maui. The impression he was giving to the new women in his life was that he was still mourning his wife and there wasn't room in his heart for another love. "We put his search program on pause for some grief therapy sessions and then some date coaching, which included plenty of role-playing conversations that have helped Neil focus on the present. He is now having a wonderful time traveling to all sorts of exotic places that he and his wife would never have gone to." Your spouse would not have wanted you to be unhappy for the rest of your time on earth. So acknowledge what you've had the good fortune to create: good health, a loving marriage, and possibly a lot more. No one can take these or the loving feelings you have for your deceased spouse away. Think of your marriage as a particularly rich and rewarding chapter in your autobiography and allow yourself to experience a new kind of love experience in this next chapter.

How Do I Begin to Find Mr. or Mrs. Right?

2

Any great relationship begins with the relationship you have with yourself. Coming to know you—your core beliefs, the way you approach life, your patterns—is the best preparation for getting to know another.

Getting to Know Yourself First

Let's take an honest look at you. I'm going to ask you to really look at yourself: who you are, where you come from, what your values are, and what you are looking for in a partner. This will take a little time but the benefits of excavating your core qualities and past patterns and enumerating your ideal desires will help you find a person who is just right for you. The more truthful you are, the more beneficial.

1. Make a List of Your Great Qualities
These are the qualities you feel particularly good about in yourself. This list will flaunt your desirable attributes. It's what makes you special. Be as complete and detailed with this list as possible. Following is a sample list to help get you started.

Great Qualities:

(Some of these qualities are only considered great to certain individuals and are negative for others, so you have to interpret this list according to your values. For example, being educated may be a great quality for one person but irrelevant to someone else. So pick the top five or so key qualities that would best describe you.)

- Accomplished
- Active
- Accepting/respectful
- Adventurous
- Affectionate
- Articulate
- Best friend
- Caring
- Committed
- Communicative
- Cultured
- Down-to-earth
- Educated
- Faithful
- Family-oriented
- Feminine/masculine
- Fun
- Gentle
- Good listener
- Happy/cheerful
- Honest/sincere
- Humorous
- Independent
- Industrious
- Integrity
- Intelligent
- Introspective

- Irreverent
- Kind
- A leader
- Loving
- Loyal
- Nurturing
- Old-fashioned
- Organized
- Passionate
- Playful
- Positive
- Quick-witted
- Refined
- Relaxed
- Religious
- Responsible
- Romantic
- Secure
- Sexy
- Spiritual
- Spontaneous
- Spunky
- Strong
- Stylish
- Successful
- Sultry
- Thoughtful
- Understanding
- Witty

2. Make a List of Your Difficult Qualities

These are the qualities that tend to cause problems in your life. They are the ones you usually try to conceal, especially when meeting someone new. Be as truthful as possible, but not brutal. It's important to be aware of these difficult qualities, so you can work to balance them with your great qualities. Following is a sample list:

13

Difficult Qualities:

Some of these qualities are only considered difficult by certain individuals, so you have to interpret this list according to your values. For example, being reserved may be a difficult quality for one person and desirable for someone else. So pick the top five or so key difficult qualities that would best describe you.

- Arrogant
- Cheap
- Chronically late
- Critical
- Defensive
- Depressed
- Dishonest
- Disorganized
- Disrespectful
- Distant/not affectionate
- Egocentric
- Exaggerate the truth
- Fearful
- Hold a grudge
- Humorless
- Irresponsible
- Judgmental
- Lazy
- Needy
- Negative
- Not communicative
- Obsessive
- Paranoid
- Passive aggressive
- Possessive
- Quiet
- Reserved
- Self-involved

- Shy
- Sloppy
- Spacey
- Standoffish
- Tardy
- Weak

3. Parental/Familial Patterns and Relationships

The way you think about and view relationships has a lot to do with the relationships you experienced in your family growing up. Your parents are your role models for what an intimate relationship looks like—harmonious or combative, supportive or critical, affectionate or distant. The point here is not to judge your parents, but rather to see how they consciously or unconsciously influence the type of partner you choose. Since each of us tends to be more like one parent than the other, it is the other parent we seek in a grown-up relationship. So, if I am more like my mother, who was emotionally distant, independent, and reserved, I will likely seek someone like my father who was hardworking and outgoing, with a wide social network and a big hug for everyone. The key here is to figure out how your parents related so that you can be aware of how this early modeling behavior affects your current relationship/partner choices. Following is a childhood history survey to help you see more clearly what factors from childhood are contributing to your current partner choices.

Childhood History Survey

1. Where did you grow up?
2. Are your parents still together?
3. If yes, how long have they been married?
4. What was your parents' relationship like when you were growing up?
5. What is their relationship like now?
6. What was your mother like?
7. What was your father like?
8. If your parents got divorced/separated, how old were you?
9. If your parents divorced, did they get remarried?

10. If so, what were your step-parents like?
11. How was their relationship, and how did it differ from your parents' relationship?
12. Where there any other adults living in the house?
13. What was it like growing up in your home?
14. Do you have any siblings? How many? Ages? Are they married? Do they have children?
15. What do/did your parents do for a living? Did they enjoy their work?
16. What is your relationship like with your family? Are you close? Is family important to you?
17. How often do you speak with them?
18. How often do you see them?
19. What is their ethnic origin? First generation?
20. What were their parents like?

This may seem like a long, involved list, but this is where you came from, these are your experiences, and this is your model for relationships. So it is crucial to really reflect on these experiences and understand the way they shape your views on what relationships are and how you feel about them.

4. Past Dating Patterns

The types of people and relationships you have been drawn to in the past can be extremely illuminating. You may not be aware of being attracted to the same key qualities over and over again because the package they are presented in can look so different. This is why it's helpful to actually write down the names of all your past partners and ask yourself, honestly, what worked and what did not work in these relationships.

Breaking Old Patterns

Make a list of all your old dating patterns that you would like to change on the left side (along with the name of that partner) and all the desired qualities you would like in a mate on the right side. This chart will help clarify old patterns that no longer work and at the same time give you some key attributes you need to start looking for in order to make better partner choices. There are few things that are harder than breaking a lifetime of patterns. So be patient and at the same time try not to be extreme and make a 180-degree turn in your desired attributes. That would be too much of a change and, in the end, hard for you to tolerate. For example, if you dated someone who was emotionally distant, don't list someone who is constantly available and whose life revolves around you 24/7. This new-found availability may cause you to run screaming from the relationship because you are not used to it. Making slow, moderate changes is more realistic. Look for someone who is not a workaholic and distant but not available 24/7 either. Try to create more balance. This will create a gradual, more comfortable change that may have a better chance of sticking.

Old Patterns	**Desired Attributes**
(for example, dating unavailable people, workaholics, abusive partners, etc.)	(for example, an attentive partner, a communicator, caring and nurturing, passionate, etc.)

Now fill this in as truthfully as you can. Are you drawn to partners who are bubbly, mysterious, and emotionally unavailable, or kind, caring, and nurturing?

If, for example, the person you most recently dated was emotionally distant and you felt isolated and abandoned, then you need to think about choosing a more emotionally available partner. In addition, if you have needy on your list of difficult qualities, it's important to assess how much your neediness contributed to your feelings of abandonment. In other words, it may be helpful to work on changing both your choice in partner and your responses to your partner's behavior. So in this case, choose a partner who is a little more available and start to work on being more fulfilled from within.

Acknowledge the Pattern

After completing this exercise, if you see a pattern emerge, acknowledge this pattern as an issue to be worked on and remedied. Let's say, for instance, that in past relationships you consistently felt your needs were not being met. Acknowledge this pattern and take responsibility for it by starting to figure out how to meet some of these needs on your own. You may want to focus on structuring your life based on nurturance and dependability. Take care of yourself; get plenty of sleep, eat healthy meals, exercise. This way there are fewer demands on your potential partner because you are meeting some of your own needs. This frees up your partner to give more generously what he or she is comfortable giving. The end result is that you'll feel much more fulfilled and happier in the relationship. So figure out what your core needs are and start to meet them on your own.

5. Ways You Approach Life

Your attitude and the way you approach life has a lot to do with who and what you attract into your life. Let's look at some different approaches and what these approaches tend to attract.

GUARDED and DEFENSIVE: If you have your guard up, people are not going to feel comfortable approaching you. You are definitely limiting your pool of wonderful potential mates. Whether you're shy or afraid of being hurt, other people are likely just as scared. It's time to open up and take a chance. What is the worst thing that could happen? It probably isn't as bad as being alone for the rest of your life. So let down those defenses and welcome in the people who are anxious to meet you.

ENTITLED/IMPOSSIBLY HIGH EXPECTATIONS: If you approach life as if people owe you something, you are going to miss out on a lot of opportunities. Likewise, if you are dismissive of people because you feel more important, then you may be blind to how great some of the people in front of you actually are. And don't forget, the person you're dismissing may have a friend or relative who is perfect for you. So, please avoid prejudging anyone.

UNWORTHY: If you have a tendency to feel undeserving, chances are you are an extremely kind, introspective type. Be careful not to let these feelings of unworthiness blossom, because they'll only work to create a barrier that is hard for others to penetrate. Read back through your list of great qualities and as you focus in on qualities you like about yourself, think about sharing these amazing qualities with another. Others will feel really lucky to have you in their life.

OPEN and POSITIVE: People who are open and positive approach the world as an opportunity. They are accessible and not at all intimidating to others. They are both appealing and find others appealing. So keep in mind that the more open and approachable you are the greater the likelihood that you'll find great people to date.

HAPPY-GO-LUCKY/SOCIAL BUTTERFLY: Social butterflies are gregarious, fun loving, happy people. They tend to be the life of the party. These happy-go-lucky types love everyone and everyone loves them, yet they have trouble settling down with any one person. They are so busy flitting around that an intimate relationship with one person can be too much for their short attention spans.

FLIRTATIOUS: When you approach people with a flirtatious attitude, you are letting it be known that you're paying attention and are available to engage in a meaningful way. People who make eye contact and smile, nod in acknowledgment, are curious, interact, and engage are fun to be with. By making eye contact with each and every person you pass in a day—whether in person, in your car, or on public transportation, you are letting them know you are available. Practice flirting every chance you get: with babies, dogs, service people—anyone and everyone you encounter. Take every opportunity to engage with members of the opposite sex, pay attention, and flirt. Rest assured your positive, open, flirtatious aura will attract attention!

"Flirting is being friendly and playful and allows you to begin to get to know someone on an intimate level."
—Anne Teachworth, matchmaker and
author of Why We Pick the Mates We Do

Getting to Know Your Ideal Mate

Now that you've taken a close look at yourself, it's time to focus on who you want to be with. Looking at your list of great qualities and difficult qualities, your family history, your past dating patterns, and the way you approach life, let's get specific about characteristics that are important to you and will complement you in a partner. People often arrive in my office with a shopping list of requirements: he must be at least six feet tall but no taller than six feet two inches, have an athletic build but not too much muscle, make over two hundred thousand dollars a year, have all of his hair, hold a graduate degree from an Ivy League school, be social, drive a high-end car, have his own friends, be a good cook, wear designer shoes, etc. These lists can be exhausting and limiting. The longer and more specific your list of must haves, the more obstacles you are placing in the way of finding a great partner. I encourage everyone to open up preconceived notions and be as flexible as possible about their requirements for an ideal mate. For example, instead of insisting that an ideal mate has a degree from an Ivy League college, put down that you want someone who is extremely intelligent. And instead of earning over two hundred thousand dollars, make note that you want someone who is financially responsible and comfortable.

1. Must Haves
Go ahead and list your top five must haves.

Lisa Clampitt's Five Must Haves:
- Extremely intelligent
- Ethical/trustworthy
- Offbeat sense of humor
- Playful
- Handsome to me

Are these ideal partner qualities realistic considering who you are? Do they balance your qualities in a realistic way? I have introduced clients to people who fit all their ideals and yet when they actually meet the person it just does not click. This list will help as a starting point of qualities a person must have and act as a sorter for you. But this sorting does not account for chemistry. Try to be a little flexible but don't throw away your "must have" list in place of chemistry, especially if the list is realistic and hits key requirements. Beware of the lure of chemistry. Your "must have" list keeps you on track and away from the temptation of pure chemistry. If you meet someone whom you really lust for, your "must have" list can go out the window. This may seem like a good idea at the time, but is usually only a short-term fix. Your "must have" list tends to help you focus on people for long-term compatibility.

2. Deal Breakers
Quite simply, deal breakers are relationship stoppers. "They are those issues people are not willing to budge on," explains Jill Weaver, owner of the New Jersey franchise of Matchmaking International. "For example, a potential match may meet all of my client's requirements—all but the deal breaker. Therefore, I will not introduce them."

Sample list of deal breakers:
This is just a sample list of common deal breakers. There can be many more, and they can be specific to each individual. Take a look at this list

and see what deal breakers are here that are deal breakers for you. Also look at this list and see if you have any of these qualities. If you do, make sure you are not disqualifying yourself from meeting someone great by being on someone else's deal breakers list.

- Rude and/or pretentious
- Self involved/talks only about self
- Poor manners
- Superficial
- Constantly late
- Heavy drinker/drug user
- Smoker
- Not well groomed, not clean shaven
- No aspirations
- Not motivated in one's career
- Lazy
- Cheap, overly concerned about money
- Short and insecure
- Dishonest, untrustworthy
- Pet or children hater
- Overweight
- Balding with a comb-over
- Bad skin or teeth
- Different religion
- Multiple divorces
- Bad breath/poor hygiene

Narrow Down the Big Picture

I recommend approaching your search for the ideal mate in the same way you look for an ideal job. First write a list of all your must haves and deal breakers. You could have twenty of each. Now really focus and distill this list down to five of each. Get rid of the extraneous details—for example, instead of large lips, dark hair, brown, or soulful eyes state that you want someone who is attractive looking to you. This helps you open up to different types of people and allows you to see through to a person's core values. If you can't get past your overly detailed surface requirements, then you're building a wall around yourself that you may never be able to scale. Let that wall down and allow wonderful, diverse people into your life. You may be surprised to notice that your life partner is already in your life—you just couldn't see them. This happened with Keith and Laurie. I set them up and they seemed to enjoy each other's company. However, Keith had this nagging thought in the back of his mind that although Laurie was one of the kindest women he had ever met, she could be a little boring. Regardless, they dated casually for about three months, and finally Keith decided that Laurie was not the girl he ultimately wanted to end up with, so he broke it off. One night he was out with his friends at a bar, he looked around, and it dawned on him that he wanted to be with Laurie. He said to himself, "What am I doing here, wasting my life in bars with friends when I could be with her?" Once he committed to her one hundred percent, Laurie felt confident enough to finally open up and Keith discovered a fascinating side of Laurie that he had never seen before. He fell in love, asked her to marry him, and they are one of the happiest couples I know.

With a greater knowledge of yourself and the kind of mate you're looking for, you can begin to attract wonderful people into your life. Be friendly and engaging wherever you go. Try smiling at five people you don't know each and every day. This not only puts you in a better frame of mind, it opens you up and makes you approachable. You'll be surprised at how many people you attract into your life.

23

Why Would I Need a Matchmaker?

3

Love—finding and keeping it—seems to be more complicated than ever before. We no longer live in small villages where families know and are known to each other. Society and individuals are less fixed and less nurturing than in the days of our forebearers. You practically have to be a relationship expert to navigate today's dating world but ironically, people are left to their own devices when it comes to finding partnership. The feeling of being in it together, the sense of community that bound our ancestors together, is all but gone from our love life. We are expected to be our own experts. Yet how can we be experts in one of the most complicated areas of life?

What Is a Matchmaker?

A matchmaker is someone who brings two people together in the hopes of arranging a compatible long-term relationship or a marriage. While today the notion of marriage includes feelings of romance, attraction and love, this has not always been true. Throughout history, a union between a man and his wife was arranged with financial gain, societal status, and/or family lineage in mind—not spiritual connection or soulful passion. In fact, bringing people together in marriage used to be a simple exchange—my cow for your daughter. Today, pairing two people together to form a fulfilling union is a coveted skill requiring delicate attention, in-depth understanding, and formidable powers of intuition.

> *"Matchmakers embrace, value, and wholeheartedly believe in their ability to seek and find love for others."*
> —*The Matchmaking Institute*

Matchmaking Throughout History

For centuries, a matchmaker served as the facilitator of what in essence was a business transaction of the highest magnitude. The marriage that resulted, at times among partners who had never set eyes on one another, was a pragmatic one meant to concentrate power and wealth, secure lineages, and consolidate properties. It was the ultimate diplomatic tool. Keep in mind that arranged marriages were especially important in dowry-based inheritance systems where women only inherited male wealth at the time of marriage, making parents particularly attentive to their daughters' matches. Even today, wealthy European merchant families continue to marry into impoverished noble families in order to obtain a coveted title.

We all remember the colorful, meddling "yenta" in Joseph Stein's Broadway play, *Fiddler on the Roof.* First came marriage then—hopefully—came love. Communities relied on experts to pair up their young: the wise, well-respected Nokado in Japan; the Portador in Mexico; the Kalyn in Russia. In medieval Catholic society, matchmaking was considered a function of the village priest. Similarly, in Orthodox Jewish communities, the Shadchan was and continues to be responsible for setting people up in marriage. He researches and makes inquiries into the character, financial status, family background, and degree of religious observance of prospective partners. He even serves as a physical and emotional boundary keeper at the beginning stages of the dating ritual—helping to iron out any problems that arise.

In America during the mid-1800s, mail-order brides became popular among pioneers heading west to settle on the open, untamed land. These men needed hardy women prepared to work hard. So, they advertised in newspapers to find wives willing to brave the harsh conditions. And today with the advent of the Internet, mail-order bride sites are proliferating offering women from Russia, the Ukraine, Kazakhstan, Uzbekistan, the Philippines, Thailand, and many other less privileged countries.

Likewise, in almost fourty African and Middle-Eastern countries, a go-between such as a family member or town elder arranges marriages for underage females. In India, China, and Japan, a significant number of marriages continue to be arranged by family members. It's fascinating to note that while India has perhaps the most arranged marriages, it also has one of the lowest divorce rates of any country in the world. This certainly suggests that the individual touch of matching personalities, interests and, integrating families makes for a strong and lasting relationship.

> ### *Today the matchmaker is viewed as more of a professional headhunter for the heart than a meddling yenta.*

Today in America, love is viewed as an inalienable right. Finding a life partner is added to people's "to do" list along with paying the credit card bill and booking that much-needed Caribbean vacation. Americans can be as discriminating about their love choice as they are about finding the right apartment, job, or pair of shoes. So, rather than wait patiently for Mr. or Mrs. Right to arrive, people are searching for love where they search for everything else—online. Online dating started with America Online in the early 1990s. In 1995 Match.com took the helm with numerous others trailing in its wake: Jdate, Yahoo! Personals, eHarmony, Lavalife, and more. While statistics show that many people enjoy surfing the net for a date, the success ratios remain unclear. And while online dating sites have become great at targeting specific niche markets, e.g., religions, careers, hobbies, etc., there are many complaints about authenticity and safety. In fact, reports abound of made-up profiles, false or out-of-date photos, and lies people have no problem typing. Many people miss the personal aspect of "old-fashioned" dating. So in a way, the obsession with online dating has spawned a keen interest in the more current concept of offline dating.

Instead of being introduced by the village elder, unmarried men and women today attend "singles" events, go on dating game shows, participate in reality television shows, and take part in speed dating. Yet the most effective of all offline dating options is matchmaking. Why? Because people value the personal touch and want the sense of community a matchmaker can bring into their lives. As human beings, we innately want to share our lives with another, and matchmakers have been making that desire a happy and fulfilling reality for thousands of years

"One year of working with a qualified matchmaker can be more effective than a lifetime of relationship hunting on your own."
—Lisa Clampitt

The Pros and Cons of Internet Dating

Before finding a certified matchmaker, many people try online dating. If you want to give online dating a shot, by all means do so. I just ask you to be careful and remember that the people you are interacting with are strangers. Following is a list of the positive and less-than-positive aspects of online dating that I want you to be aware of first.

Pros
- Easily accessible from any PC, twenty-four hours a day.
- Good way for travelers to meet singles at various destinations.
- Builds your social network by allowing you to search for and meet like-minded people.
- Worldwide medium so you can meet people all over the world.
- Inexpensive way to browse an unlimited number of single men and women.

- Offers good flirting practice.
- Free anonymous e-mail accounts.
- New video dating and voice personals help you get more of a sense of the person.

Cons

- Photos can be out-of-date or inaccurate representations.
- Dishonesty abounds—made-up profiles, exaggerated claims, married people posing as single, and more.
- Chemistry can not be determined online.
- Inexpensive up front, but the cost of going on numerous poorly-matched dates adds up fast.
- A "qualified lead generator"—nothing more.
- Safety can be an issue. Remember, you're dealing with total strangers, so be sure to limit the amount of personal information you reveal online and always meet your date in a public space.

Modern-Day Matchmakers

Life isn't as simple as it used to be. We take on too much both at work and at home and feel incredible stress trying to get everything done yesterday. When the stress becomes overwhelming, we hire help: personal organizers, personal trainers, personal shoppers, personal pet care providers, and more. Today's matchmakers are personal trainers for your love life. They bring you together with people you would never otherwise meet and guide you through every step of the dating process to ensure that finding your soul mate is as fun as it is rewarding.

Ways a Matchmaker Adds Value

- Works with you to understand your past and how it affects your current dating patterns.
- Helps you change outmoded or unproductive thinking patterns.

- Suggests altering specific behaviors to reflect more of what you want in your life.
- Builds self-esteem by focusing on your strengths.
- Packages and presents you in the best possible light
- Markets you to a well-defined target community
- Prescreens all potential dates for you
- Follows up after each date for specific feedback—pluses and minuses
- Zeroes in on your perfect match using your feedback

"Matchmaking is an art form, a talent, a skill," explains Steven Ward, matchmaker and owner of Master Matchmakers in Philadelphia. "If someone has a unique lifestyle, situation, career, or family, and needs to meet a uniquely compatible individual to complement these things," continues Steven Ward, "this someone could benefit from hiring a matchmaker. If someone wishes to expedite their search for an ideal match, is jaded, bitter, or disillusioned by the dating game and would like some personal representation, direction, guidance, and support, they will welcome the assistance of a matchmaker."

Why Use a Professional Matchmaker

Professional matchmakers are experts in the field of helping people find love. They get to know you one-on-one, coordinate dates, and guide you through the process of finding the right relationship.

> *When working with a professional matchmaker you can expect to make some kind of meaningful connection within the first three or four introductions.*
> —*Lisa Clampitt*

Trust. Matchmakers make it their business to get to know you: your wants, needs, and desires. It is important for them to establish trust so that you feel comfortable communicating all your wishes.

Privacy. Your matchmaker will only introduce you to people you're interested in and will not release your contact information or photo to anyone without your permission. By using a matchmaker, no one—not your boss, your ex, or your family members—will know you are looking for a mate unless, of course, you tell them.

Safety. No one wants to meet a perfect stranger. Your matchmaker has spoken with, met and checked the references of everyone you are introduced to. Because of this, you can explore romance without fear or worry.

Personalized Service. Your matchmaker gets to know YOU, and based on your unique personality, lifestyle, likes, dislikes, and values, understands exactly who will be a suitable and rewarding match.

Time Saver. You don't have to spend countless hours browsing thousands of online profiles, writing dozens of introduction e-mails, and spending the evening alone when a promising prospect doesn't show up for a date. Your matchmaker takes care of all the details for you, allowing you to save your energy for the actual date.

Personal Screening

Matchmakers meet personally with each person you are introduced to to determine common relationship goals, values, interests, and must haves. In this way, matchmakers are able to match based on these important criteria. If friends match you up with someone, they probably won't be as objective about personality and character aspects because they'll want you to like their friend. "The most important benefit a matchmaker offers is screening. Today, it's easy to gain access to available singles online, however, there is no way to know whether what they present is true," reminds Leora Hoffman, owner and founder of Leora Hoffman Associates in Bethesda, Maryland. This professional screening adds a feeling of safety to the dating experience that is irreplaceable, along with knowledge and objectivity. "The computer has cut us off from real people and real feelings," says Jennifer Forde, a matchmaker at Great Date Now in Purchase, New York. "When I was a kid, there were social gatherings and block parties and adults were always having cocktail parties. I look around and everyone I know works until seven in the evening, heads home to eat, watches television, gets the kids to bed, and then plunks down in front of the computer to 'socialize' with others. They use e-mail, chat rooms, instant messages, message boards, Internet dating, and now even 'winking' to make contact. If someone winked at me on the street in real life, I'd assume he's a pervert and move on. However, I am told this 'winking' is the highest form of flattery in the new cyber-palace of dating. What do I know? I am just a matchmaker who deals with flesh and blood people whom I have seen, run background checks on, and gotten to know personally. People need to be proactive, get out and stop hiding in cyberspace where Prince Charming may really be a perpetrator. A good, reputable matchmaker can be the safest way to meet someone new and appropriate."

What Can I Expect When Working With a Matchmaker?

4

Matchmakers are professionals who make it their business to find you the right relationship. In order to do this successfully, they take time getting to know you and what you're looking for. Matchmakers understand that people may feel uneasy about seeking help with their love life. Love is meant to happen naturally, so it's no surprise people feel uncomfortable seeking professional help in this most important area of their life. "I'm here for when those 'chance' meetings just haven't happened, for those who don't like the feeling of being 'out there' on the Internet, for those who are more comfortable one-on-one than in large social meet-market settings," explains Julie Ferman, Certified Matchmaker and owner of Cupid's Coach in Oak Park, California. "I offer a dignified shortcut to meeting pre-qualified relationship-minded single people. It's the same principle for hiring a real estate broker or an employment agency. You're just hiring yourself a heart hunter."

The Process

Working with a matchmaker is a rewarding journey that puts you in the driver's seat of your love life alongside a supportive, encouraging, knowledgeable guide. "Matchmakers have tremendous dating prowess which they lend their clients," says Steven Ward, owner of Master Matchmakers. Rest assured, with a professional matchmaker at your side, you'll enjoy the ride!

The Initial Phone Call

This call is one of the most proactive steps you can take. Your matchmaker should immediately put you at ease. He or she knows how difficult this initial phone call can be and will ask you a few fairly innocuous questions. These questions are meant to evaluate if they are the right person for you to work with. Be prepared to answer the following:

- What is your name, phone number, and age?
- How did you hear about our service?
- What do you do for a living?
- Have you been married before?
- If so, are you divorced?
- Do you have children?
- What are your relationship goals?
- What are you looking for in a mate?

Since matchmakers tend to specialize in different markets, i.e., specific religious groups, age ranges, sexual orientations, geographic areas, etc., the answers to these questions help them ensure a good fit for you. If, for example, this matchmaker only works with men under forty and you're a fifty-two-year-old male, she'll tell you so immediately and hopefully be able to recommend a matchmaker who works with over-forty male clients. Set aside twenty minutes for the initial phone conversation and be prepared to set up a face-to-face meeting.

The Initial Appointment

This initial appointment will last approximately one to two hours.

Arrive looking your best, as you would for a job interview or a date. The matchmaker will notice your appearance, the way you talk, your body language, and more. This visual information will help your matchmaker start piecing together your style and who you are. No need to feel nervous—this time is for you and you alone. Just be yourself and answer questions as honestly as possible. Be prepared to answer the following initial questions about your last relationship:

- What was he or she like emotionally and physically?
- Was it love at first sight?
- Were you friends first?
- Were you opposites or alike?
- What did you like about him or her?
- What didn't you like about him or her?
- How and why did it end?

Your matchmaker will encourage you to open up and begin the process of really learning about yourself. For instance, he or she may ask, "Why are you single? Have you been proactive in your search? If so, in what ways? If not, why not? What is your type? I had a wonderfully attractive female client a few years ago who told me she went out all the time and realized there just weren't any good men out there. When I asked her about the circumstances of her going out, it became clear that she liked to go out with a group of close female friends which made it virtually impossible for her to be approached by a man. She then told me that when she was out with her friends, she didn't really like men approaching her—it embarrassed her. So in her case, it was important to look at why she wasn't allowing herself to be available.

Your matchmaker will go through your relationship history, activities you like, your values, and will compile a list of your deal-breakers and must-haves. Some may also give you a personality test to help zero in on your personality type. Remember, matchmakers will not be matching likes and dislikes the way online sites and dating services do. Instead they match personalities to personalities and values to values.

"The Internet brings quantity, Matchmakers bring quality"
—*Charlee Brotherton,*
Brotherton & Associates Introductions, Inc.

The Actual Matching

Your matchmaker will pull together all the information gathered at your initial meeting and begin to think about matches for you. He or she will call you to discuss a few matches, sharing professionally prepared profiles and often pictures. Different matchmakers have different ways they work, so ask your specific matchmaker what information you will receive about your matches and if you get to see pictures. According to Diane Bennett of Cinema Suites, "I have photos of all my clients and the men pick pictures of the woman whom they would like to meet. I don't do blind dates, he sees her photo and some information and she gets the same, plus they both speak to me about each other before an introduction is made." So you select and agree on one or two potential matches, and the matchmaker will talk to both of you about the other. If you would then like to meet each other, a date is set up, either by the man calling the woman or by the matchmaker—whatever is most comfortable.

Feedback

The matchmaker calls both parties after the date to hear feedback—both positive and less than positive. These honest responses are the most helpful way your matchmaker has of narrowing in on exactly what you want in a partner. It also helps the matchmaker guide you in successful dating strategies. If for example your date's feedback was that you talked too much about work and your ex, that's important and helpful feedback for your next date. Your matchmaker will help you steer clear of these kinds of conversation stoppers and equip you with great conversation starters before you go out on your next date. Likewise, if you have sex on the first date, you probably aren't taking the time to really get to know each other and discover if you have common goals and values. Remember, dates are explorations and feedback from both parties is an essential part of the reality check. Your matchmaker keeps a detailed record of each date you go on, when it occurred, who called whom, and all your feedback. "I have found having lunch with my client after each of their first few introductions allows me to get to know the client better, receive feedback on the dates, and slip a little date coaching in between the main course and dessert," says Charlee Brotherton, a certified matchmaker of Brotherton & Associates Introductions, Inc. and owner and CEO of the Singles Station in Tulsa, Oklahoma.

Additional Benefits

As relationship experts, Matchmakers provide you with so much more than pre-qualified introductions to potential partners. They also work with you in a number of different ways to help you learn more about yourself and what you are looking for and to help you grow throughout this exciting journey.

"Matchmaking is a holistic process that looks at the whole you."
—*Lisa Clampitt*

Personal Cheerleader

Your matchmaker is your very own personal cheerleader—in your corner every step of the way. He or she listens carefully to all you say about yourself, what you're looking for, and your responses to each and every date. If you liked a particular date and that date did not like you, your matchmaker can explain why. You are never left hanging or wondering. Often a date not liking you has more to do with his or her family history than with you. Remember, we are all attracted to what we are used to from our past. Yet being aware of how you act on a date is very important information for you to have and learn from. Based on feedback, your matchmaker will let you know if the way you are being perceived on a date matches up with the way you would like to be perceived. Your matchmaker also remains positive and helps you build self-confidence as you get out there and date. If for any reason you start to feel discouraged, your matchmaker is there to remind you of just how special and unique you are.

> *"A matchmaker's job is to allow each person to be their own advocate, to open up, be confident, be positive, and feel good about themselves."*
> *—Lisa Clampitt*

Personal Consultant

As wonderful as your personality may be, those horn-rimmed glasses might make you look outdated. Your matchmaker will alert you to quick, easy fixes you can make to present yourself in the best possible light. You may look twice as nice with whiter teeth, more flattering clothes, or an up-to-date hair cut. Whether it's dating tips, fashion advice, or etiquette training, your matchmaker is there to help. According to Julie Ferman, owner of Cupid's Coach, some of the most common mistakes people make on dates are talking too much, interrupting, picking up cell phone calls, complaining about exes or family members, allowing the eye to wander, dressing too casually, talking about sex, and not being up-front about their current and long-term goals for dating. To put your best foot forward, Julie recommends looking for all that is lovely and right about each person you meet, say YES more often, engage in conversation, and primp—care about your hair, what you wear, your physical fitness, and appearance.

Provide Added Exposure

Matchmakers get you out there dating. Dating, like everything you do, takes practice. Your matchmaker will help you with a variety of skills, from opening up your parameters to great conversation starters. "When I first met Tara," says Julie Ferman, "she was firmly rooted in her belief that the right man for her would be tall, very successful, Christian, he'd have a full head of hair, a washboard stomach, and his car would be even nicer than hers . . . She's become a sponge for the learning and coaching I've offered to her, and she's thoroughly enjoying opening up her parameters, experiencing what she calls '31 flavors of men,' and she's completely refined her deal-breakers and must-have list. She's learning so much about herself and about men. Tara is having a blast and she calls her investment with my company the 'best money she ever spent!'"

Great Conversation Starters

- What are some of your favorite vacation spots?
- What is your favorite room in the house?
- What do you love doing on Sunday mornings?
- Who was your most influential family member?
- If you could redo your schooling and career, what would you study and what career would you pursue?
- If you had a million dollars to give to charity, which one would you choose?
- Who from history do you admire?
- Who are your mentors?
- If you could spend next Saturday in New York City, what would you do there?
- Extend a compliment.

How to Choose Your Matchmaker

5

T he best way to choose a matchmaker is the same way you choose any professional in your life—whether it's a doctor, lawyer, or accountant. Let's say, for example, you suddenly lose sight in one eye. You will immediately seek out the best ophthalmologist (eye specialist) you can afford. The same is true with a matchmaker. You want to find a highly reputable matchmaker who specializes in the type of person you are and whose fees fit your budget. For example, if you're a thirty-four-year-old woman who wants to have children, you wouldn't choose a matchmaker who specializes in women over fifty. Look for the most highly regarded professional in the field who has a style you like and can offer exactly what you need at a price you can afford.

What Style Works Best for You?

Every individual has his or her own personal style—make sure the matchmaker you select has a style that works for you. The better you know yourself, the more easily you will recognize a matchmaking style that is comfortable for you. While doctors have a bedside manner, matchmakers have a matching style. Consider the following styles.

Nurturing

Do you want someone who has a kind, gentle, encouraging manner? Matchmakers with a nurturing approach are great listeners who will help make you feel good about yourself each step of the way—from the first getting-to-know-you meeting to every dating feedback conference. A nurturing matchmaker will provide kindly phrased, helpful advice to make it easier for you to open up and feel cared for throughout the dating process. Rob Anderson of Club Elite in New York City works to create a comfortable and safe environment, often one of the few places where his clients feel completely at ease and able to let their hair down. He knows that life and dating can be hard enough, so he wants his clients to feel comfortable and encouraged about being the best they can be. He makes them feel great about themselves not only on the dates he sends them out on, but in their everyday world as well. Rob knows that the better people feel about themselves, the more attractive they are to others and the more successful they will be in finding love.

> *"Keep in mind—matchmakers are NOT therapists."*
> *—Lisa Clampitt*

Direct

Are you a busy, let's-get-this-done type of person? Do you like to know exactly what is on the table and make fairly quick decisions with the input of a professional? If so, then you may feel most comfortable working with a matchmaker who doesn't adorn the facts, just presents information to you in a timely, honest manner and seems to know immediately whom to set you up with. According to Janis Spindel, a professional matchmaker in New York City, "All my clients are *very busy* men who are *very picky* and hire me to do the editing for them. I am incredibly successful because I match entirely on premonitions and never attempt to fit a square peg into a round hole."

Go-Getter

Are you looking for a real go-getter who will aggressively market you? Do you want a matchmaker who checks in with you almost daily, goes through candidates, and tells you how best to proceed? If so, you may want a matchmaker with a hard driving style. Leora Hoffman, president and founder of Leora Hoffman Associates in Bethesda, Maryland, likes to get a complete psychological, family, and relationship history of her clients before beginning the matching process. Then, as a practicing attorney with eighteen years of experience in the matchmaking business, she uses her well-honed instincts to suggest potential matches. Once people meet and like each another, she employs her legal skills to advocate strongly for and negotiate the success of the match.

Holistic

Are you looking for someone to take a lot of time getting to know you— excavating your past and truly understanding all that goes into making you the unique person you are? Do you want someone who is able to really listen, take in, and formulate a clear picture of you from what you share about yourself? Then you want a matchmaker who is comfortable sitting with you and coming to know you in your entirety. Kailen Rosenberg, president and founder of Global Lover Mergers and The Elite Love Registry, LLC in Minneapolis, Minnesota, takes her work as a matchmaker and "love architect" very seriously, knowing that healthy relationships begin only when two "healed and emotionally healthy" people are involved. Kailen is after much more than just connecting two people in marriage. Through her uncanny way of "knowing" just who is meant to be with whom, she matches people she knows are emotionally healthy enough and have a knowledge of just "how" to have a healthy relationship. She coaches along the way, helping detect and clean up any opportunity for sabotage, and she also acts on each client's/couple's behalf once they are engaged and sometimes even after they are married, to ensure they stay in a place of growth for themselves as well as the relationship. Kailen is known by her clients as a "soul mate" and life design expert.

"Don't just get involved with someone . . . Hire a matchmaker and get evolved in your next relationship."
—Anne Teachworth, author of
Why We Pick the Mates We Do

Interviewing Matchmakers

Following is a list of questions to ask each matchmaker you interview. Listen carefully to their answers and you will begin to get a sense of their specific style. The answers to these questions will help you hone in on which matchmaker is right for you.

Questions to Ask Matchmakers

- How long have you and/or your company been in business?
- How many matchmakers does the company have and how long have they been working with the company?
- What are the matchmakers' qualifications and background?
- How are clients screened and interviewed?
- Does the matchmaker meet everyone in person, including potential matches?
- How do clients get matched up?
- Who does the matching?
- Do clients get to see an in-depth "profile" or bio along with a photo?
- How does the company advertise and attract new clients?
- How many clients are in the database?
- What is the cost and what do I get for my money?
- Is there a minimum and/or maximum number of matches that I can receive?
- What is the cost for renewing?
- Is everyone charged the same fees?
- If I meet someone I am interested in dating, can I put my contract on hold?

- Do you provide client references or have client testimonials?
- How does communication between client and matchmaker take place, e.g. phone, e-mail?
- What are the business hours and am I able to speak with my matchmaker after hours?
- Are there photos and letters from happy clients?
- How successful are the matchmakers? How does your company define success?

Invaluable Matchmaker Qualities

While each matchmaker has his or her own individual style, there are three important qualities that we feel are necessary for all matchmakers to have in abundance.

Trustworthiness

You only want to work with a matchmaker you feel is extremely honest and trustworthy. You want to trust their taste, their opinion, and their ability to get to know you and help you find an appropriate partner. Listen carefully to the way they answer your questions. Are they over-hyping their service or being truthful? Do they boast an unrealistic success ratio? Stating that ninety percent of clients marry within the first three introductions may be a bit over inflated. Are they explaining the actual matching process to you in the detail you want? Or are they vague in regard to information you want? Do they seem to be promising too much based on your past experience—the ease or difficulty you have had—attracting partners? Do they promise marriage in a year? Over-promising can be a red flag to make note of when screening potential matchmakers.

A recent client told me he had previously worked with a matchmaker who promised to find the love of his life in three months. This set up an expectation that was perhaps a little unrealistic and understandably, my client was extremely disappointed when this promise was not fulfilled. A lack of trust was created in their relationship that made it difficult to continue working together. Finding a great relationship may take time. Be patient and don't be lured in by the promise of immediate results.

Non-Judgmental

It is extremely important for matchmakers to listen to all you have to say—family and past dating history, what you like, and what you're looking for—without judgment. In your interview, make sure the matchmaker is mirroring what you say or writing it down in an open, objective manner. It is their job to gather information, not to judge. Pam Stowell, owner of Lunch Appeal in Liverpool, New York, describes what a client can expect when working with her, "A very professional, discreet atmosphere where the client can share what is important to them in a relationship and in a mate. We don't judge We understand who they are and whether they are looking for someone to mirror them or complement them. We understand people come to us for various reasons. We hand-select matches after meeting everyone one-on-one and get feedback from each introduction."

"Matchmakers come from a place of curiosity—not judgment."
—*Lisa Clampitt*

Communication Skills

Strong communication skills are essential in a matchmaker. Find out how information will be communicated between you and your matchmaker. Do you sit down in the office with the matchmaker on a regular basis? Or, after the initial meeting, does communication take place mainly by telephone and e-mail? How much and what kind of feedback does the matchmaker supply after each date? Is he or she available to talk 24/7 or only during business hours? Does your matchmaker listen well or does he or she ask the same questions over and over? Is this person able to summarize what you have told him or her and what you are looking for? Can your matchmaker offer you a game plan at the end of the first meeting? Do you feel that he or she truly understands you, your lifestyle, your goals, and your history? Is this person going to be able to represent you accurately to your matches?

It is also extremely important that a matchmaker sets up periodic reviews. This is where you sit down together and go over exactly what's worked, what hasn't worked, rearrange goals, and update the business plan for your love life. This kind of open, reflective communication is essential.

Ability to Attract What You Want

The matchmaker you choose to work with *must* be able to attract the type of partners you are interested in meeting. Before signing a contract, ask about the type of clients he or she currently has? Let's say you're a fifty-year-old woman and you are interested in meeting younger men. Is this something the matchmaker has the ability to do for you? Have they worked with clients similar to you and your desires? If so, were they successful? How do they attract their clients—advertising, recruiters? Can you look at some profiles they have in mind as a sample? How optimistic are they about the chances of finding exactly what you want? A particular matchmaker may be wonderful for you in a number of ways, but keep in mind the most important feature—having access to potential partners that interest and excite you.

Remember, who you choose to be your matchmaker is a very important decision. This person is going to be involved in one of the most important aspects of your life. You are going to have to trust your matchmaker and share a lot of personal information that you may not have shared with many people. You need to be able to believe in his or her ability to search and find the type of people you are looking for. The more you trust your matchmaker and the more honest and open you are with him or her, the more successful your journey will be. So do you homework and choose wisely.

How Can I Get the Most Out of Using a Matchmaker?

6

Prepare well. Do all the homework in chapters one, two and three before your initial appointment. Make lists of your great qualities, your difficult qualities, your past dating patterns, and the way you approach meeting people in your day-to-day life. I'm going to encourage you to begin opening up a little in all areas of your life. Shake off some of that stubbornness or those impossibly high expectations. Let down your defensive wall and begin to flirt—make eye contact, smile at strangers, be approachable, accessible, and fun.

> *"Flirting is being friendly and engaging."*
> —*Anne Teachworth*

Prepare for Your Appointment

Refine and distill down your list of Must Haves and Deal Breakers as explained in chapter two. Likewise, bring your family history, past relationship pattern sheet, and the itemized list of your great qualities and difficult qualities. The more information you provide about yourself, the more successfully your matchmaker will be in understanding you and representing you to others. For example, it may be obvious that you are good-looking, successful, interesting, social, and well-mannered. However, let the matchmaker know about your special qualities that aren't quite as noticeable. For example, are you passionate about the environment, do you love to cook, are you politically active? Are you loyal, ethical, and honest to a fault? These are qualities that comprise a person's personality, and are what your matchmaker uses to find your perfect match. Matching personality traits and values along with common relationship goals is the basis for a successful, long-term relationship. It's nice to have common interests too—but common interests are not as critical as sharing personality traits and common values. So provide your matchmaker with a detailed explanation of your personality and values—what's important to you and what you're especially passionate about.

Have Your Matchmaker Keep You on Track

Ask your matchmaker for a schedule to follow and have him or her check in with you periodically to keep you accountable. Did you call and make a date with one of your potential partners this week? If not, why not? What's holding you back? Be honest with your matchmaker. If you have trouble making the first call to arrange a potential date, let your matchmaker know. He or she may be happy to call and arrange the first date for you. My client John told me specifically that he wanted to be married by Christmas, which gave us eight months. Although I am not a huge fan of imposed dates, I let him know that we both needed to work hard to find him someone great. The first few introductions were not exactly right. They fit all his criteria but the chemistry was just not there. Then I met Jessica and I knew intuitively that she would be perfect for John. I called him, told him about Jessica and how I felt she was a great match for him. I gave him her telephone number and stressed that it was important he call her right away. When I checked in with him a few days later to see if they had gotten together, it turned out he hadn't even called her. By the time he finally did call Jessica, she was insulted that it took him so long to call her and didn't want to meet him. When I asked John about his not calling, he said that he gets so busy at work that he loses track of time.

He asked if I could help. I told John that the next time, I would find out his schedule ahead of time and arrange the date so all he would need to do is show up. This actually worked very well for him and he didn't miss any other opportunities. Keep in mind, your matchmaker is there to help you find the love of your life, but you also have to be proactive and accountable.

Alert Your Matchmaker to Your Strengths and Weaknesses

It's best to let your matchmaker know exactly what your strengths and weaknesses are so they can accentuate your strengths and also help you with any weaknesses. For example, if you aren't feeling particularly good about some aspect of yourself, let your matchmaker know. He or she is there to help in all areas of your love life. My client Fred felt very self-conscious about the fact that he didn't go to one of the top law schools. He was defensive about it and afraid that women wouldn't be particularly impressed or attracted to him because of it. I'm so glad he was able to be honest with me about his insecurity because the truth about Fred was that he was a wonderful, genuine, loyal, accomplished man. The fact that he was a lawyer with a great job at a top law firm was enough for anyone to be impressed by. He was also well-mannered, tall, and attractive. The only person who didn't see him as terrific was Fred. The more we looked at his positive qualities, the better he began to feel about himself and as a result the more confident and relaxed he began to feel on dates. The important thing is to get out there dating. So, be sure to alert your matchmaker to any problems you may feel you have so he or she can help you work through concerns, insecurities, and weaknesses that just seem to keep getting in your way. Your matchmaker is there to guide you to success.

Let Your Matchmaker Know How You Like to Work

Do you prefer to meet in person? Or are e-mail and telephone conversations easier for you? Can you talk during the day or only after work? Do you want the matchmaker to call you before each date and prep you? Would you benefit from some pre-date coaching? Or do you prefer the matchmaker only contact you after each date for a full debriefing? Make sure your matchmaker takes notes on the feedback you give after each date and keeps it in your file. You will want to review your progress every three to six months. Tell your matchmaker up front if you want to meet in person for these progress reports so you can schedule it.

Reality Check

Is what you are presenting what you want to present? Oftentimes we think we're coming off funny and quirky but really we come off aggressive and odd. Through coaching, your matchmaker will help you gain insight into how others see you and how you behave on dates. With feedback, you can create more consistency between how you come off and how you want to be seen. Your matchmaker will help you behave in a way that attracts more of what you want into your life. You may want to attract a specific type, so think about the specific traits you want to have shine through. I had a client who wanted to attract an elegant and sophisticated woman who would admire his success. So he would spend entire dates talking about his travels around the world and his success. He thought he was being impressive but his dates felt he was totally self-involved and uninterested in them. He had no idea that this was the impression he was giving. It wasn't until he received this reality check from his matchmaker that he let go of the act and became more himself on dates—attracting the type of women he really wanted to be with.

Be Honest

For some, talking openly about their personal, inner psychology is not easy. You may be afraid of such exposure with a stranger. I urge you to view it in the light of sharing personal information about yourself with someone who will not judge you, but instead will try to help you by providing honest and open feedback. This feedback from your matchmaker is invaluable. Sometimes it can be hard to hear. For example, my client Susan is a painter and likes to dress in a creative, artsy way. The feedback I kept receiving from the men she liked was that they thought she was sloppy and unkempt looking. We talked about how she was presenting herself on these dates, and it turns out she had paint under her nails and wore dresses made out of a natural fiber that she thought made her look unconventional and interesting. In fact, they were unflattering in just about every way, according to her dates. Susan had a wonderfully slender, curvaceous figure, so when she began dressing in a more stylish way that showed off her figure, the feedback from her dates was great. She began to feel much more confident and her true personality was able to shine. So, while nobody likes to hear they are doing something wrong, it's important to listen to the feedback your matchmaker provides. Trust me, if you can allow yourself to take in constructive feedback from your matchmaker, you will gain valuable information.

How Does a Matchmaker Find You a Match?

7

The Contract

You and your matchmaker will sign a contract that specifies exactly how the matching will work. There are two basic types of contracts.

Number of Introductions

You can purchase a specific number of matches. If your matchmaker likes to work this way, be sure to also include in the contract a time period over which these matches or introductions will take place. In other words, if your contract specifies ten matches, make sure these will take place within a specific amount of time such as one year. After all, you want the introductions that you paid for in what you feel is an acceptable amount of time.

Time Period

Many contracts specify a time period during which you will be working with your matchmaker. The most common contracts are either six months or one year and include unlimited introductions during that time. The time period approach allows the matchmaker enough time to really do a quality search for you. To be on the safe side, it's a good idea to include in this type of contract a minimum number of introductions, say, six for a six-month contract or twelve for a twelve-month contract. Any reputable matchmaker will be happy to write a minimum number of matches into your contract.

Matching Techniques

To follow are some of the things your matchmaker may be looking at in order to determine suitable matches for you.

Relationship Goals

For a match to take root, both partners must share similar relationship goals. According to Charlee Brotherton, certified matchmaker and owner of Brotherton & Associates Introductions in Tulsa, Oklahoma, "two people need to be heading down similar paths with similar goals to ultimately make a life together." The similar path Charlee is referring to begins with what any two people are looking for in a relationship. If, for example, one person wants to get married and have children and his or her perfect match based on values, interests, life experience, and more has just emerged from a long-term marriage with four children, they are not likely to have similar relationship goals and therefore would not make a good match. "It's critically important to be mentally ready to accept a relationship—if you truly aren't ready, then the best match in the world will never get beyond a few dates," says Scott Stowell of Lunch Appeal in Syracuse, New York.

Values/Partner Qualities

Are you a loyal, trustworthy person who loves children? Or a workaholic who wants to lead a luxurious, jet-set lifestyle? While these two quite different people may meet and be extremely attracted to each other, they would have a hard time negotiating a successful relationship. A matchmaker would not put these two people together. Your matchmaker may have you fill out something such as a potential partner qualities worksheet similar to the one below so as to match you with a partner based on these important qualities and values. For example, if you are extremely passionate and sexual, you will want a partner who shares that quality and wants passion in his or her life. Likewise, if you are really close to your family, have strong family values, and like to spend a lot of time with family members, your matchmaker will pair you with someone who shares your strong sense of family.

Item	Not Essential	Somewhat Important	Moderately Important	Extremely Important
Ambitious				
Career-oriented				
Casual lifestyle				
Community activist				
Conservative-minded				
Creative				
Culture-oriented				
Dependent				
Enjoys conversation				
Extrovert				
Family-oriented				
Flexible				
Sexual/passionate				
High energy				
Independent				
Introspective				
Introvert				
Liberal-minded				
Loves cats				
Loves children				
Loves dogs				
Lower energy				

Luxury lifestyle				
Morally liberal				
Morally strict				
Organized				
Outdoorsy				
Physically active				
Playful				
Politically active				
Rigid/firm				
Social drinker				
Spontaneous				
Sports oriented				
Successful				

This is a sample of the type of form your matchmaker may use to hone in on the personality qualities you are looking for in a potential partner. Please indicate the level of importance to you.

Once you've filled out the worksheet, your matchmaker may ask you what the most important qualities are to you. They will match you based on those especially important qualities/values. Let's say they are: Education, Religion, Family, Healthy/active lifestyle and Passionate/sexual. Your matchmaker will introduce you to potential partners who share these critical qualities.

Interests

Matchmakers focus more on their client's goals, values, and personality qualities than on common interests. While it's wonderful to enjoy doing the same kinds of activities and share common interests, doing so does not predict long term compatibility. In fact, this is one of the problems with most online sites—they match people based on interests rather than the more important qualities and values inherent in each individual. If you are a fanatic about an activity and it is extremely important that a partner at least likes and respects that activity, then be clear about that with your matchmaker. For example let's say you are a competitive sailor and have a beautiful thirty-eight foot sailboat that you love to race, you may not want to be matched with someone who gets seasick easily. While your matchmaker will have you fill out a worksheet on your interests, they only need to see two or three interests in common to proceed with a match, as long as the more important personality qualities and values line up.

This is a sample of the type of form your matchmaker may use to establish what common interests you and a potential partner share. Please rate them according to your interest level.

Item	No Interest	Some Interest	Would Go/Do	Like It	Love It!
Alpine skiing					
Archeology					
Architecture					
Art					
Auto racing					
Biking					
Bowling					
Camping					
Classical music					
Comedy					
Conversation					
Country music					
Cross-country skiing					
Dancing					
Dining out					
Fine wines					

Fishing					
Flying (private plane)					
Golf					
Hiking					
Jazz music					
Jet skiing					
Jogging					
Live theater					
Motorcycles					
Movies					
Museums					
Musicals					
Opera					
Parasailing					
Photography					
Playing cards					
Politics					
Popular music					
Racquetball					
Rap/hip hop					
Reading					
Rock music					
Sailing					
Singing					
Swimming					
Television					
Tennis					
Travel–domestic					
Travel–international					
Water skiing					
Weight training					

The Interview

The one-on-one interview is where your matchmaker collects a great deal of information about you that he or she uses for matching purposes. A matchmaker will listen to your spoken words and at the same time get a sense of what is not spoken. He or she will notice the way you speak. Are you shy or connected? Do you make eye contact when you speak or not? Are you self-deprecating or a little too full of yourself? The matchmaker will read your gestures, facial expressions, energy level, posture, and body orientation. This one-on-one meeting provides the matchmaker with a holistic look at you—in a sense exposing your true essence. Through understanding each individual's essence in combination with life goals and values, a matchmaker can successfully bring together two people, who may otherwise never meet, to enjoy a lasting relationship.

Feedback

A matchmaker collects feedback after each and every date in order to determine the fullest possible picture of you and what you are looking for. Once collected, it becomes easier to figure out exactly what is working and what isn't working in your dating experiences. This feedback is critical in zooming in on how you present yourself to another. You may be one way with your matchmaker and completely different with dates. Feedback from both you and your dates helps uncover what's really happening out there in the dating world. Often we don't present ourselves the way we think we do. And yet, how would we ever know? Matchmakers collect feedback to help you develop a successful style and hone in on the type of person you will enjoy spending the rest of your life with.

Matchmaker in Action

Patrick Perrine, founder and owner of My Perfect Partner in San Diego, California, has created what he calls the Magic 7—a seven step process for efficiently and effectively identifying the perfect match for his clients. This is a thorough, professional, and proven program he spent more than ten years developing.

Step One: *Initial Contact, Intake and Screening with Client.*
A Partner Perfect Compatibility™ Profile is completed so we can understand the preferences and desires of potential clients. The questionnaire is followed-up with a private consultation by Patrick, which establishes the important personal relationship between client and matchmaker and ensures that My Perfect Partner is the right matchmaking service for the client.

Step Two: *Review of Company Policies and Procedures, Intentions and Goals Evaluation.* Patrick personally discusses the company's policies and procedures before reviewing and signing a contract. A retainer fee is paid and Patrick begins the matching process.

Step Three: *Needs and Wants Assessment.* Client begins the in-depth personal analysis focusing on the client's past relationships, unique personal qualities, geographic location, personality type, client preferences (e.g., age, socioeconomic status, physical characteristics, commitment levels, etc.), and several other variables that are determined through analysis.

Step Four: *Potential Life-Partner Matching Process: Evaluating, Screening, and Pre-Qualifying.* Preliminarily, the Matchmaking Database selects potential life-partners for clients based on client's assessment. The database may have someone that is the right match for you immediately. If not, the matchmaker conducts a targeted search based on the client's personal needs and wants. Once a potential suitor has been selected, the president conducts an interview to determine whether or not the suitor would be a good match for the client. The screening process allows for additional insight and matchmaker intuition into the compatibility of the client and any potential life-partner.

Step Five: *First Round Introduction.* The matchmaker will present only those potential life-partners that have many of the qualities that you seek. The initial meeting with a potential mate is arranged in a no-pressure atmosphere by the matchmaker. The idea is to meet in a space with no obligation for either party, yet conducive to getting to know each other.

Step Six: *Follow-up Consultations with Clients and Potential Match.* After each date, Patrick will debrief with both the client and potential life-partner. During this debriefing the matchmaker will review the qualities presented by both parties. This information is shared with the client allowing the matchmaker and client to hone in on life-partner qualities sought out and help fine-tune the search criteria further if necessary. The matchmaker conducts monthly check-ins/reviews with the client to stay on top of dating status, satisfaction, and next steps.

Step Seven: *Relationship Consulting and Coaching.* When a life-partner is found, the client's matchmaking services end after six months of successful dating or upon marriage, whichever happens first. Dating and relationship coaching services continue for clients who have been successfully matched until the contract ends.

Remember that each matchmaker will have their own method and process. Understanding some basic ways a matchmaker works will allow you to understand the basic process, and you will then be able to ask questions. But be open to each matchmaker's individual method and style and see if it works for you. If you like what he or she has to say in the interview, hire the person and put your trust in their personal method of matchmaking.

The Method Behind
the Matches

8

Most of us use instinct or intuition when choosing a life partner. Your matchmaker will undoubtedly rely on the same feeling or "hunch" when pairing couples together. The ability for them to intrinsically produce matches will prove to be an incredible advantage to you. However, the skill of coupling can also be looked at by using a more scientific approach: employing structure and logic.

Steven Sacks, author of *The Mate Map: The Right Tool for Choosing the Right Mate,* believes that although many happy unions are created instinctually, there is a particular structure you can look at when deciding if someone is a good match for you. If you combine this more structured approach with all the elements discussed earlier in this book—looking honestly at yourself and why you are where you are in life, recognizing and breaking old patterns that have not worked, identifying qualities you are looking for in a mate, and opening yourself up to more possibilities—you'll be providing yourself and your matchmaker with critical partner selection information.

When it comes to finding true love, most people expect things to happen naturally; for a spark to one day ignite and then grow into our living happily-ever-after. Perhaps it's not really our fault that we feel this way—we see it in the movies all the time. Why wouldn't it happen for us that way? Well, from a logical perspective, this way of thinking doesn't make much sense. Life, after all, is not a fairy tale. Sacks explains that "most often people don't know what they want in a mate until they've stumbled upon the right one, or are reeling from the wrong one. So, the idea is to get people to think about exactly what they want in a relationship before they end up in one that may not be right for them."

Take It One Small Decision at a Time

Deciding whether or not a person is "the one" can seem daunting. Let yourself relax and take it slowly, one date at a time. No need to make any big decisions—just break it down into small decisions. After talking on the phone with a potential partner ask your self if you liked them enough to go out on a date. After the date, write down what you liked and what you didn't like as much. Then decide if you want to go out on another date with this person. If you take it date by date, eventually you will be lead to the larger question: is this person a potential long-term mate for me?

"Seventy-five percent of us are visual learners.
When you put things down on paper, it sinks in that much more.
So I urge you to write down your impressions after each date."
-Steven Sacks, *author of* The Mate Map

By documenting your feelings and talking about them with your match-maker, you are taking a more structured approach to love.

It also helps if you look beyond common interests. People tend to rate levels of compatibility based on the number of activities or hobbies they can enjoy together. Sacks believes this is really just a default mechanism people use when asked to describe what they are looking for in a mate. Common interests have the ability to bring two people together, but they do not carry enough weight to make a relationship successful. For example, a relationship may start with a shared passion for the theater, and then grow from there. But a relationship should not start with a common interest and continue as a result of further common interests. Certainly sharing common interests makes getting to know someone fun, but it is not a predictor of long-term compatibility. Sacks claims "people should have one or two common hobbies they can enjoy together—but this is just a part of the picture, not the main element."

Look at Profile Attributes

These attributes are the basic, factual information you need to know about the person you may like to meet. According to Sacks, there are eight main profile attributes: age, career/job, education level, ethnicity, geographic desirability, religion, socioeconomic status, and hobbies/interests. These basic requirements help your matchmaker narrow down potential partners for you. Be sure to let your matchmaker know how important each of these categories is. For example, how important is geographical location? Are you willing to date someone outside of your area? If so, how far?

Relationship Essentials

In order for two people to thrive in a relationship, Sacks tells us, people need to be compatible in four key areas: personality, physical attraction, chemistry and love.

PERSONALITY: Each person's personality is unique. Certainly, the personality fit each of us wants in a partner is different from that of every other person because there are so many attributes and so many individual desires and needs. So, it helps to be as specific as you can with your matchmaker about what personality traits you are looking for in a partner. Sacks lists important personality traits to consider: affectionate, assertive, calm, decisive, disciplined, energetic, follows rules, handles adversity well, career ambition, high maintenance, high sex drive, honesty, independent, industrious, intelligent, kindhearted, makes me laugh, neat, optimistic, private, proactive, religious, responsible, saver, sensitive, sociable, spiritual, talkative, and worldly. Think about how important each of these traits is to you.

PHYSICAL ATTRACTION: When it comes to physical attraction, everyone has a sense of their general "type." The more specific you can get with your matchmaker about physical characteristics you are looking for in a partner, the better. There are fifteen physical attributes to help you prioritize: hair, eyes, smile, lips, teeth, nose, ears, skin, height, body, sex appeal, cuteness, pretty/handsome, and overall look. All of these constitute the outer beauty of the person. So for example, is it extremely important to you that your partner have good teeth? Do you want someone with full lips? If you can tell your matchmaker the level of importance of these key physical elements, it will serve as a useful tool in helping them find you potential partners. Keep in mind, this is a starting point to help your matchmaker get a picture of your ideal match, but they will then match you based on the whole picture, so remember to try and be as flexible as possible and be open to your matchmaker's suggestions.

CHEMISTRY: It is generally thought that two people either have chemistry or they don't have chemistry. Chemistry isn't something you can plan for, but it also isn't as black and white as most people think. There are actually six different categories of chemistry. We can have a high level of chemistry with a person in one category and a low level with that same person in another category. The six categories of chemistry are: verbal communication, nonverbal communication, sexual compatibility, desire to be together, ease of getting along, and the level of influence we have with the other. You and your matchmaker can review the areas of chemistry you feel with each date to help you begin to understand what areas are important to you as well as what areas you shine in.

LOVE: If all goes well, you will find love. Love is defined as having deep feelings of affection and emotional intensity toward a potential or current mate. While it is often thought that two people are either in love or they're not, love is not as simple as that. This is because love is not just one entity, but is made up of six different categories. And like chemistry, we can have a high level of love in one category and a low level in another category with the same person. The six love categories are: what you feel, importance, what you find special (or not special), love fulfillment, love compatibility, and changes my outlook for the better (or worse). It's important to discuss these feelings and signs of love with your matchmaker as you progress in a relationship before putting your contract/membership on hold. Your matchmaker is there to help make sure a relationship is right for you. Be as forthcoming with your true feelings as you can.

What Makes a Great Match?

While it's beneficial for you to provide your matchmaker with as much personal information as possible, I also believe it is helpful for you to rely on your matchmaker's expertise. Matchmakers really do listen and understand your needs, wants, and desires. If you can let go of the need to control your love-destiny and place your trust in the hands of an experienced, professional matchmaker who looks at people objectively and matches based on core values and personality qualities, you will reap the benefits many times over.

Matches Made in Heaven

Following are quotes from different matchmakers on what they think constitutes a match made in heaven.

"Good matches come from shared values, morals, being in the same state of life, and sharing some common interests. Additionally, knowing whether you want someone who is opposite, similar, or complements you . . . . Everyone is looking for something different and a matchmaker is in the unique position of knowing what their client is looking for."
—*Pam and Scott Stowell, Lunch Appeal*

"A good match consists of common interests, friends, and goals."
—*Anne Teachworth, Perfect Mate, Inc.*

"A good match is when two individuals have the same relationship goals, some similar interests, and a true interest in learning and growing with each other. Clearly, a man who never wants children should not be paired with a woman who is looking to raise a family soon. However, an adventurous woman may indeed intrigue and complement a regimented man. It all depends, as each and every person I meet is unique. That is what is so special about being a matchmaker. Sometimes, that energy I get from one client is unmistakably "meant" for another client, and when the two meet there are fireworks from the start. Provided the right foundation of trust, respect, common interests, and chemistry exists, it just works."
—*Jennifer Ford, Great Date Now*

"Good matches are people with positive attitudes—they make long lasting relationships/commitments and eventually marry."
—*Carlita Hughes, Relationships for You*

"A good match is based on two people who are attracted to each other and who can make the right decisions to assure a lasting and loving relationship. Life is all about choices."
—*Diane Bennett, Beautiful Girls, Successful Men*

"A good match consists of common values, goals, and mutual chemistry."
—*Leora Hoffman, President and founder of Leora Hoffman Associates in Bethesda, Maryland*

"Two people who see eye-to-eye on important issues such as personal ethics, values, sex, and goals, who are also physically compatible and geographically desirable, possess a similar sense of humor and may share a passion for something, usually make for a good match. I personally don't put too much emphasis on religion, family, or politics because love trumps any of these areas."
—*Steven Ward, Master Matchmakers*

"A good match is all about chemistry. Chemistry is an intangible that no one can account for—it could be a "banter," a smile, or a smell, you never know.

—*Janis Spindel, Janis Spindel's*
Serious Matchmaking Company

"A good match consists of two people who respect and admire each other, share critical values, a few passions, are comfortable together, and are attracted to each other. The icing on the cake—both have a sincere interest and commitment to communicating with each other and to working through the challenges inherent in dating and relationships, and they can and do laugh together."

—*Julie Ferman, Cupid's Coach*

"A good match is about finding someone who is compatible, shares the same relationship goals, complements your personality, and who is a good balance for you. Also, try and find someone who you can laugh with. It is your sense of humor that will keep you going, and ice it off with the indefinable chemistry!"

—*Rob Anderson, Club Elite*

Dating Ins and Outs

9

Dating plays a vital role in the matchmaking process. This is where you get to practice. Think of it as test driving your list of must-haves and wants. If meeting with your matchmaker is more like classroom experience, dating is hands-on field experience—offering you the opportunity to get out there and find out who and what exactly works for you. You may think you know exactly what you want and how you present yourself on dates. While dating, you will find out if what you think you want is what you want and if who you think you are presenting is actually who you are presenting. Your matchmaker will supply you with invaluable feedback from each date. So, listen to your matchmaker, have fun, and practice. Incorporate the dating tips in this chapter and I guarantee your dating experience will be all the more enjoyable and successful.

Keep These Eleven Important Dating Tips in Mind as You Plan Your Date.

1. Choose the right place to meet:
Make it a quiet, neutral place convenient and accessible to both of you, outside of your home or apartment and away from noisy bars and distrac-

tions. You want to be able to communicate easily and hear all the details of the conversation.

2. Stay focused on the other person:

Avoid distractions during your date and keep in mind that this is a new opportunity to connect. Focus and relate directly to your date and listen to what they have to say. Be curious and ask follow up questions to their stories. This is especially helpful if you tend to be nervous or quiet at first.

3. Keep the conversation balanced:

Don't monopolize the conversation with a rambling, verbal resume about yourself or your accomplishments. You may think you are impressing your date, but often, talking too much on a date will make the other person lose interest and feel you are self-involved. Remember this is a date, not a job interview. Make sure it's a give-and-take and show your curious side. People enjoy talking about themselves; make sure they have a chance.

4. Be a flirt:

Flirting is a great way to show someone you are interested in them. It lets them know that you are paying attention and available to engage. Practice flirting every chance you get. Make eye contact, smile, be curious, interact, and engage with members of the opposite sex. Rest assured, your positive, open, flirtatious aura will attract attention.

5. Stay in the present:

Avoid talking about exes or any horror stories from the past. As tempting is this can be, it is a lose-lose situation. No one wants to hear you put down people, and it is even worse if you speak about your past with a negative slant. Instead, concentrate on interests or points of view you have in common. Enjoy finding out about someone new and discovering what you are like now, with this new person.

6. Be positive:

Everyone is attracted to someone who is happy. Leave your worries at home when you go out on a date. No one wants to hear about your bad day or your problems. We all have enough of our own gripes. Dating is an opportunity to go on vacation from your daily grind. Give your date and yourself a break during this time. The more upbeat and positive you feel, the more attractive and magnetic you are.

7. Don't have sex on a first date:

Showing someone you are interested or attracted to them by flirting is one thing, but maintain boundaries by leaving some mystery for the second date. Getting sexual right away doesn't usually work out. Allow yourself time to balance physical attraction with other important elements like basic values and communication, as well as discovering similar outlooks and interests. Give your date a chance to be more than just a sexual encounter.

8. Take your time:

Give yourself time to discover how you feel about this person and how they feel about you. If you tend to be intense, serious, or move very fast in relationships, this is your time to relax and enjoy getting to know someone and seeing all their qualities—especially those you may not see on the first few dates. You can't rush a relationship or take it faster than the pace at which each of you is comfortable. Enjoy savoring the moment.

9. Learn to recognize the signs of unequal attraction:

Try and learn to read the body language of your date. Look at what they are telling you both verbally and nonverbally. Try and be honest with yourself. Often the level of attraction on a date is not equal. If you sense your attraction to them is not really reciprocated, don't force the issue. If this person is not right for you, save your energy for someone who is. And if you're the one who is less interested, don't be rude but don't lead them on either. Let the other person know that you had a wonderful time but don't make plans for future dates if you have no intention of seeing them again. This may feel more comfortable at the time, but in the end it just leads the person on.

10. Follow up after the date:

If you are interested in seeing this person again, don't play games. Call them and ask them out again or return their call if they call you first. Don't make the other person guess where you stand. Be honest and communicate. This will help you both in understanding each others intentions and desires. There is nothing ruder than unreturned phone calls.

11. Try, try again:

Dating can take practice. Learn from it and don't get discouraged. The more you get out there, the more opportunity you have to meet others. When it is right, you will find that person who sees how special you are. Remember your great qualities and lead every date with those qualities you feel best about. If you feel it and believe it, it will shine through.

Dating Advice from the Experts

Professional matchmakers have a lot to say about dating. Dating is how their clients come to know one another. I guarantee that matchmakers have heard it all when it comes to dating. Based on their many, many years of dating experience and feedback, the following is what they want to pass on to you so that your dating experience is the best it can possibly be. But first let's look at what these experts recommend *not* doing on a date. Sometimes it's easier to learn from what we do wrong. Here are what matchmakers across the country say are the biggest dating mistakes.

Dating Disasters from the Experts

"The #1 dream killer on a date is to turn it into a psychotherapy session where one complains endlessly about one's past personal life. It is rude to unburden oneself in such a selfish and thoughtless manner. Both men and women are guilty of this. Of course, to the poor soul listening to this human whine machine, the speaker comes across as a gigantic loser and a sore loser at that! Remember while you're verbally attacking your former lover, the person to whom you're telling your horror stories to is the same gender and they also feel attacked and put down. There is plenty of terrain to cover without getting into your poor choice of a mate!"

—Diane Bennett

"The biggest mistakes people make on a date are not minding their manners, talking too much about religion, politics and personal finances, past relationships, family or negativity in general. Likewise, drinking to excess, commenting on others, being cheap or taking advantage of someone (i.e., ordering the surf-and-turf plus a $200 bottle of wine) is simply not nice and not acceptable."

—Steven Ward

"The biggest mistake people make on a date is talking too much about themselves."

—Scott and Pam Stowell

"The biggest mistake people make on a date is discussing their "emotional baggage." Also, people make the mistake of assuming that they will be dating this person and speaking as if they assume the date will lead to a future relationship, which is very premature and tends to put the other person off right away."

—Leora Hoffman

"Dating mistakes include talking too much, interrupting, picking up cell phone calls, complaining about exes or family members, allowing the eye to wander, dressing too casually, saying you'll call and then not calling, talking about sex, and failing to communicate clearly about the primary purpose for dating—not being up front about the current and long-term goal for dating."

—Julie Ferman

"The biggest mistake on a date is to talk about your ex—either positively or negatively."

—Anne Teachworth

"Many people make the date sound like an interview rather than a getting to know you conversation."

—Janis Spindel

Making a Date Great: Advice from the Experts

Follow these dating tips from the experts and you are on your way to dating success!

"Err on the side of possibility and look for all that's lovely and right about each person who crosses your path (instead of what's missing, wrong or lacking). Say YES more often, engage in conversation with "strangers" all the time, don't wait for invitations, rather YOU be the one to extend them. Primp—care about your hair and what you wear and your physical fitness and appearance.

—Julie Ferman

"Go back to basics—he pays for the date, she listens to his every word as if he is the most interesting man in the world. She looks sexy and wears lovely perfume, the restaurant is romantic, his car is clean, his nails are clean, he is stylishly attired with a decent haircut, no one complains (OK politics), he offers to pick her up (no 50-50 driving), the conversation is not an inquisition but natural and fun and easy (how much money he earns and whether she had a boob job are none of anyone's business), she pays attention to him, does not constantly look over his shoulder to see who's coming in the door, she flirts and smiles (American women desperately need flirting lessons), no one discusses their pets or kids (stop it—boring in the extreme!). Women—be interested not interesting! Very important, competition he can get at the office, so cut it out! He leads, you follow . . . or girls, go get a young, broke boyfriend and you boss him around!"

—Diane Bennett

"I believe that the golden rule for dating should be as simple as the golden rule for living, 'Treat others the way you wish to be treated.' Always be yourself and let your date do the same. Be tolerant of others, but speak your mind respectfully. The best relationships are forged when two individuals understand and applaud their own individuality, but can come together to work toward a common goal. Make no mistake, any great relationship got that way with a lot of work and understanding. Nothing worth achieving comes too easily . . . in life or love."

—Jennifer Ford

"Be positive at all times no matter how dire a situation may get. Men, take charge but take a woman's input into consideration. Give her options and at least let her think she's got a say in things. Women, allow the man to feel secure. Be amenable, and regardless of his initial impression, give him a chance to impress you. Be frank but be polite. If something is bothering you, bring it into the open. If questioned about religion, past relationships, politics, personal finance, family, or anything else that may be considered sensitive my suggestion is to be candid, be honest, but be evasive. There are far more things to discuss on a date that will increase the likelihood of making it a step further. Men, dress to impress. Nice shoes, a nice watch, a good haircut and outfit will immediately earn you consideration for a second date. Women, remember, *all* men are visual creatures. Don't go out dressed for the office. Accentuate your best features and remind everyone that sees you out on your date that you are a vibrant, attractive, confident, sexy woman."

—Steven Ward

"If what you are doing isn't working then you need to try something different. Try to get out of your comfort zone. Take it slow; make sure you have agreement on both sides before you get totally involved with each other. Typically, one party is driving the relationship at a much faster pace. Slow down and make sure your partner is happy being a co-pilot."

—Scott and Pam Stowell

"Go out with someone four times before you decide the person is not for you. I don't believe in first impressions."

—*Anne Teachworth*

"Be open and receptive—go out on a first date with an open mind. Be yourself. If there is not an immediate physical attraction, don't worry. It sometimes takes a while to fall in love and at the end of the day it's personality that really counts. We all age and change, and it is what is underneath that counts the most and will carry you through life."

—*Rob Anderson*

Best First Dates

These are just a few of the hundreds of stories matchmakers have shared with me to inspire you.

"I had to lean pretty hard on Steve to call Marilyn. He typically wanted to date women younger than him and Marilyn was the same age. I felt strongly that he would really enjoy meeting her. He acquiesced after my persuasion. He called her rather late to set up their coffee date and said, "What are you doing now?" Marilyn had already settled in for the night, taken off her make-up, was in her pajamas but, as her profile states, "is spontaneous." True to form she said, "What the heck, sure I want to meet you now!" So they each headed to rendezvous for their coffee date at a local restaurant. They closed the place! The feedback in my in box from each of them was that they were equally smitten. They were inseparable for months and I recently attended their wedding reception. Steve was glad he listened to his matchmaker!"

—*Nicole Leclerc*

"I had a new client named Cindy—a beautiful Christian woman who worked as a special education teacher. On her very first match I introduced her to a physical therapist named Bill. Bill was a strikingly handsome, Christian, single parent raising a handicapped son. They made a beautiful couple on paper and everyone in my office was excited about this introduction. Lo and behold, we got a call from Cindy and we could hear the excitement in her voice. Bill had just called her and they realized they had a mutual friend who had mentioned perhaps setting them up. Why the friend hadn't, I don't know. As we suspected, Cindy and Bill hit it off and have been dating ever since. We got a call a few weeks ago telling us that they had set a wedding date!

—*Charlee Brotherton*

"Scott was a forty-three-year old physician who had grown tired of the typical first date over dinner and twenty questions. He was really excited to meet Lisa, whose Cupid's Coach personal resume showed him not only her beautiful photos, but what she loves to do for fun. On her list of passions were: roller coasters, pinball, people-watching, and eating "kid food," like hotdogs, snow cones, and popcorn. Scott had a blast planning their first date at the Santa Monica Pier. He and Lori fell in love over air hockey, arcade games, pepperoni pizza, and one large cotton candy."

—*Julie Ferman*

You now know a lot about yourself, about finding your perfect partner, what a matchmaker does, and how one can help you in your quest for love. We also want to provide you with a list of matchmakers. Look over this list that follows and take note of how each particular matchmaker works. They are all different, so you will want to evaluate, based on all the information in this book, which matchmaker or matchmaking company appeals to you and your individual style. Call some of these matchmakers and interview them over the phone. Keep in mind that shopping for a matchmaker is like shopping for any other type of expert. Don't rush. Do your homework. Ask questions. And most of all, enjoy the process of finding a matchmaker who will help open your heart to the love of your life.

PART II

*Guide to
Introduction Services
and Matchmakers*

Note to the Reader

H ere is a selection of matchmakers and introduction services in the U.S. and Canada, with each company's process, clientele, location, and other vital statistics.

Please note that this survey has been conducted as independent research, free of any advertisements.

The Matchmaking Institute does not endorse any specific matchmaker. This survey has been compiled to give the reader more knowledge of different services available.

Please send your feedback and reviews on any matchmaker and introduction service to **www.matchmakinginstitute.com/survey**

Survey Methodology

Pricing:
$ = under $1,000
$$ = $1,000 - $2,500
$$$ = $2,500 - $5,000
$$$$ = $5,000 - $10,000
$$$$$ = $10,000 +

Qualification:
CMM= Certified Matchmaker
CSW= Certified Social Worker

Category:
Dating, Coaching, Relationship, Marriage

Service:
Personal Search, Members to Members, Members to non Members

Market focus:
Professionals; Elderly; Divorced; Community, if any; Ethnicity, if any (African-American, Asian, Asian-Indian, Caucasian, Hispanic/Latino, Middle Eastern, Native American); Religion, if any (Buddhist, Christian Hindu, Muslim, Jewish); Sexual Orientation, if any (Gay Men, Lesbians)

Serving:
1) main office; 2) other areas

Pre-screening:
Yes or No (Clients and/or Matches)

Show pictures:
Yes (male only, female only, both)

Credentials:
Matchmaking Institute's Professional and Certified Matchmakers Network Member

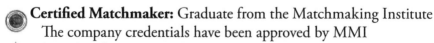

Certified Matchmaker: Graduate from the Matchmaking Institute
The company credentials have been approved by MMI
(Matchmaking Institute)
The company is a Member of the BBB
(Better Business Bureau)

Matchmaker Survey by State

USA:

Arizona	Kelleher & Associates
	Selective Search
Arkansas	Singles Station Dating Company
California	Beautiful Girls–Successful Men/Millionaires Matchmaker
	Cupid's Coach
	Distinctive Search
	Kelleher & Associates
	Lavender Liaisons
	My Partner Perfect
	Pretty People International
Colorado	Ignite Matchmaking Service
	Introductions
	It's Just Lunch
Connecticut	Catherine's Connections
	Great Date Now
	VIP Life

District of Columbia	Distinctive Search
	Elite Love Registry
	My Partner Perfect
Florida	Catherine's Connections
	Elite Introductions
	Kelleher & Associates
Georgia	Options
	Traditional Matchmakers
Illinois	Kelleher & Associates
	Selective Search
Indiana	Matchmaker International
Iowa	Compatible Connections
Louisiana	Perfect Mate
Maine	The Matchmaker
Maryland	Distinctive Search
	Leora Hoffman Associates
Massachussetts	Catherine's Connections
Michigan	Matchmaker International
Minnesota	Global Love Mergers
Missouri	Preference Introductions
	Selective Search
Nevada	Elite Love Registry
	Kelleher & Associates
New Hampshire	The Matchmaker
	Together of New Hampshire
New Jersey	Catherine's Connections
	Great Date Now
	Master Matchmakers
	VIP Life

New York	Catherine's Connections
	Club Elite
	Denise Winston Professional Matchmaker and Love Coach
	Great Date Now
	Janis Spindel Serious Matchmaking
	Lunch Appeal
	Master Matchmakers
	VIP Life
Ohio	Dating Directions
	Lunch Date
Oklahoma	Singles Station Dating Company
Pennsylvania	Date Nite
	Master Matchmakers
	Options
South Carolina	The Relationship Company
Tennessee	Matchmaker International
	Singles Station Dating Company
Texas	Kelleher & Associates
	Selective Search
Vermont	Compatibles
Virginia	It Takes 2
	Options
Washington	Elite Love Registry

CANADA:

Dinner Works
Like Fine Wine
Misty River Introductions
Real Connections

Kelleher & Associates Inc
Amber Kelleher
Established in 1986
Located in Scottsdale, AZ
P: 800-401-MATCH (6282)
E: info@kelleher-associates.com
W: www.meettheelite.com

Category: Dating; Coaching; Relationship; Marriage
Company Motto: Exquisite matchmaking since 1986.

At a glance:
- Service: Clients to Clients; Clients to Members
- Age range: Male clients: 25 and up; female clients: 25 and up
- Market focus: Busy Professionals and Affluent Entrepreneurs Nationwide
- Serving: 1) Scottsdale; 2) California, Chicago, West Palm Beach, Dallas, Las Vegas, and New York
- Pre-screening: Clients: Yes; Members: Yes
- Show pictures: Clients: Yes; Members: No

Background/Bio:
The ultra-exclusive mother-daughter matchmaking team of Kelleher & Associates was founded by Jill Kelleher in 1986. Kelleher & Associates caters to an exceptional clientele. Noted as a National Search Firm, we represent the best and brightest in the U.S. as well as abroad. We are distinguished by our stellar reputation, priority on discretion, and a proprietary database, resulting from over two decades in our industry. Boasting a staff of over 30 full-time matchmakers nationwide with domestic offices that include New York, San Francisco, Beverly Hills, Scottsdale, La Jolla, West Palm Beach, Dallas, Las Vegas, Chicago, and Silicon Valley.

Process/Personal Style:
Once an applicant is successfully accepted, Kelleher clients are provided with a very unique, personalized service like no other. Each of their introductions are hand-selected with great detail and are based on their client's specific criteria. Kelleher & Associates set the standard for matchmaking over 20 years ago, and continues to do so today.

Pricing/Service: $$$$ to $$$$$
Includes: One full year of quality introductions, with additional year of hold extensions. Custom memberships may also include relationship experts, psychiatrists and life coach.

Credentials: BBB

91

Selective Search, Inc.
Barbie Adler
Established in 2000
Located in Phoenix, AZ
Phone: 866-592-1200
E: barbie@selectivesearch-inc.com
W: www.selectivesearch-inc.com

Category: Coaching; Relationship; Marriage
Company Motto: Elite matchmakers to the most eligible, commitment-minded bachelors.

At a glance:
- Service: Clients to Members
- Market focus: affluent professionals
- Serving: 1) Phoenix, AZ; 2) Chicago, New York, Los Angeles, Orange County, San Francisco, Atlanta, Dallas, Miami, Washington, DC, St. Louis
- Number of Clients (paying): 100; Members (non-paying): 50,000
- Pre-screening: Clients: Yes; Members: Yes
- Show pictures: Clients: Yes; Members: upon request

Background/Bio:
Barbie Adler, founder and president of Selective Search, one the leading off-line personal matchmaking firms with clients across the country, is one of the industry's most respected matchmakers, sought after lifestyle management coach, and personal relationship expert. Profiled as an authority on relationships by *Forbes, Fortune, The Economist, The Wall Street Journal, USA Today, Self, Men's Heath,* and CNN, among others, Barbie's expertise in the matchmaking world is in high demand.

Process/Personal Style:
Exclusive within the industry, Selective Search represents a new paradigm in matchmaking, that of the "executive recruiter." The approach, the process, and the results are unique to Selective Search and are a testament to Barbie's vision of helping individuals find each other in a very personal, yet effective and efficient environment.

Pricing/Service: $$$$$
Includes: One year membership, ten introductions

Credentials: MMI Network Member

Singles Station Dating Company
Charlee Brotherton, CMM
Established in 1979
Located in Bentonville, Fort Smith and Little Rock
P: 501-255-LOVE
E: info@singlesstation.com
W: www.singlesstation.com

Category: Dating; Coaching; Relationship; Marriage
Company Motto: True Love Starts Right Here!

At a glance:
- Service: Clients to Clients
- Age range: Male clients: 25 to 85; female clients: 21 to 80
- Market focus: Professionals, Christian, and Secular
- Serving: 1) Little Rock, Bentonville and Fort Smith, Arkansas; 2) Tulsa and Oklahoma City, OK, and Nashville, TN
- Number of Clients (paying): 10,000; Members (non-paying): 100
- Pre-screening: Clients: Yes; Members: Yes
- Show pictures: Clients: No; Members: No

Background/Bio:
The Singles Station Dating Company has a 25-year reputation of helping discerning singles find romantic companionship. They have introduced more than 100,000 couples and are responsible for thousands of successful relationships and marriages.

Process/Personal Style:
They meet with potential clients for a personal interview in their offices. Clients complete a comprehensive profile and a personality profile. In addition they are screened for felony convictions, history of mental illness and drug or alcohol abuse. After every introduction, each client calls with feedback of their date to member services and decides if they would like another introduction or continue to date the person they just met.

Pricing/Service: $$ and up

Credentials: Member ⬤ of the Professional and Certified Matchmakers 🅱🅱🅱 of the Board of Directors of the Network

Beautiful Girls – Successful Men/Millionaire's Matchmaker
Dianne Bennett
Established in 1992
Located in Beverly Hills, CA 90210
P: 310-859-6929
E: dianne3562@yahoo.com
W: www.diannebennettmillionairematchmaker.com

Category: Dating: Coaching; Relationship; Marriage
Company Motto: Men are attracted to what they see.

At a glance:
- Service: Clients to Members
- Age range: Male clients: 30–65; female clients: 18–55
- Market focus: Successful and/or beautiful people
- Serving: Southern California
- Number of Clients (paying): 75 men; Members (non-paying): 1000+ women
- Pre-screening: Clients: Yes; Members: Yes
- Show pictures: Clients: Yes; Members: Yes

Background/Bio:
Dianne Bennett always had the ability to introduce men to women that they could date or marry. A matchmaking company was born from that skill.

Process/Personal Style:
Men view female clients' photos and select the girls that they want to meet. I represent over a thousand gorgeous girls.

Pricing/Service: $$$$$

Credentials:

Cupid's Coach
Julie Ferman, CMM
Established in 2001
Located in Oak Park, CA 91377
P: 877-345-LOVE; 805-371-9557
E: julie@cupidscoach.com
W: www.cupidscoach.com

Category: Dating; Coaching; Relationship; Marriage
Personal Motto: Bringing people together with high tech and high touch.

At a glance:
- Service: Clients to Clients; Clients to Members; Clients to Subscribers
- Age range: Male clients: 30-85; female clients: 22 -65
- Market focus: Relationship-oriented professionals
- Serving: 1) California; 2) free private national registry
- Number of Clients (paying): 600; Members (non-paying): 2,000
- Pre-screening: Clients: Yes; Members: Yes
- Show pictures: Clients: Yes; Members: Yes

Background:
Julie Ferman is Cupid's Coach. A matchmaker, dating industry consultant, media personality, professional speaker, singles event producer, and writer, Julie founded her personal matchmaking service, CupidsCoach.com in 2001. With over 1,000 marriages to her credit, she knows the love business, and has heart and soul dedication to the industry.

Process/Personal style:
The Cupid's Coach process begins with either online registration directly on the site or a telephone interview. New members are encouraged to attend one of Julie's seminars or events, as well as a 90-minute in-person consultation. During that consultation, the new member will have an opportunity to see who's in the community and at that point, make an intelligent choice as to whether or not to move into a more proactive search program.

Pricing/Service: $$ to $$$$
Includes: Professional photos, in-person consultation, a minimum of one introduction per month, no maximum.

Credentials: Member of the Board of Directors of the Professional

Distinctive Search, Inc.
Teresa Ann Foxworthy
Established in 1996
Located in San Francisco and San Diego, CA
P: 888-800-1241
E: info@originaldatingcoach.com
W: www.matchmakercoach.com & www.originaldatingcoach.com

Category: Dating; Coaching; Relationship; Marriage
Company Motto: Attract and keep the love of your life!

At a glance:
- Service: Clients to Members
- Age range: Male clients: 25+; female clients: 25+
- Market focus: Marriage-oriented professionals
- Serving: 1) San Francisco Bay Area/San Diego Area; 2) Baltimore, Washington
- Number of Clients (paying): 10; Members (non-paying): 3,500+
- Pre-screening: Clients: Yes; Members: Yes
- Show pictures: Clients: Yes; Members: Yes

Background/Bio:
Teresa Ann Foxworthy founded Love in the 21st Century to offer distinctive search matchmaking introductions and original dating coaching programs for professionals ready to meet and keep the love of their life! Her background includes a counseling practice of 17 years, life coaching for over 10, and pioneering in the field of personal transformation for over 20 years.

Process/Personal Style:
Ms. Foxworthy's clients are invited to a complimentary 30-minute consultation to get acquainted with her and her programs. Matchmaking clients are delighted by her caring yet savvy approach to get results fast. Her first objective is seeing how ready clients are for dating or marriage and then understanding what kind of person would be the best match for them.

Pricing/Service: $$$ to $$$$
Includes: 6 introductions in 6 months; 12 introductions in 12 months; 2-hour orientation consultation; and much, much more.

Credentials: MMI Network Member

Kelleher & Associates, Inc.
Amber Kelleher
Established in 1986
Located in Sausalito, CA 94965
P: 800-401-MATCH (6282)
E: info@kelleher-associates.com
W: www.meettheelite.com

Category: Dating; Coaching; Relationship; Marriage
Company Motto: Exquisite Matchmaking since 1986.

At a glance:
- Service: Clients to Clients; Clients to Members
- Age range: Male clients: 25 and up; female clients: 25 and up
- Market focus: Busy professionals and affluent entrepreneurs nationwide
- Serving: 1) Scottsdale; 2) California, Chicago, West Palm Beach, Dallas, Las Vegas, and New York
- Pre-screening: Clients: Yes; Members: Yes
- Show pictures: Clients: Yes; Members: No

Background/Bio:
The ultra-exclusive mother–daughter matchmaking team of Kelleher & Associates was founded by Jill Kelleher in 1986. Kelleher & Associates caters to an exceptional clientele. Noted as a National Search Firm, we represent the best and brightest in the U.S. as well as abroad. We are distinguished by our stellar reputation, priority on discretion, and a proprietary database, resulting from over two decades in our industry. Boasting a staff of over 30 full-time matchmakers nationwide with domestic offices that include New York, San Francisco, Beverly Hills, Scottsdale, La Jolla, West Palm Beach, Dallas, Las Vegas, Chicago, and Silicon Valley.

Process/Personal Style:
Once an applicant is successfully accepted, Kelleher clients are provided with a very unique, personalized service like no other. Each of their introductions are hand-selected with great detail and are based on their client's specific criteria. Kelleher & Associates set the standard for matchmaking over 20 years ago, and continues to do so today.

Pricing/Service: $$$$ to $$$$$
Includes: One full year of quality introductions, with additional year of hold extensions. Custom memberships may also include relationship experts, psychiatrists, and life coaches.

Credentials: BBB

Lavender Liaisons
Susan Adams
Established in 2006
Located in Campbell, CA 95008
P: 408-375-2111
E: susan@lavenderliaisons.com
W: www.lavenderliaisons.com

Category: Dating; Coaching; Relationship
Company Motto: Elite matchmaking exclusively for lesbians

At a glance:
- Service: Clients to Clients; Clients to Members
- Age range: Female clients: 28–65
- Market focus: Professional lesbians
- Serving: 1) San Francisco/Silicon Valley Bay Area; 2) will grow in California, nationally and hopefully internationally in 5 years
- Number of Clients (paying): 50; Members: (non-paying): 100
- Pre-screening: Clients: Yes; Members: Yes
- Show pictures: Clients: Yes; Members : No

Background/Bio:
Following a decade of successful matchmaking in the straight world, Susan chose to re-direct her expertise to the gay community! She refined her recruiting skills by matching clients with aligned work environments that supported their work-styles and potential. Now she has combined both areas of expertise to match only the most compelling, attractive, healthy lesbians with their lifetime partners!

Process/Personal Style:
Susan personally meets with every client. She customizes her approach and introduces her client to members who meet her criteria, while actively recruiting from gay community events—sporting, political, outdoors enthusiasts, artistic, and cultural until her client finds her partner. Feedback following each date refines her search and assists her clients insight. Her goal is lifetime partnership.

Pricing/Service: $$
Includes: 1 year to 18 months with unlimited intros, relationship coaching, access to relationship workshops mediated by our licensed therapist, and singles events.

Credentials: Member of the Rainbow Chamber of Commerce

My Partner Perfect
Dr. Patrick Perrine
Established in 2004
Located in: San Francisco, CA 94101
P: 415-358-6868; 877-225-5928
E: matchmaking@mypartnerperfect.com
W: www.mypartnerperfect.com

Category: Dating; Coaching; Relationship; Partnerships
Company Motto: Not everything in life is temporary

At a glance:
- Service: Clients to Members
- Age range: Male clients: 25–75;
- Market focus: Exclusively gay men
- Serving: Clients nationally
- Number of Clients (paying): No more than 30 at a time; Members (non-paying): thousands
- Pre-screening: Clients: Yes; Members: Yes
- Show pictures: Clients: Yes; Members: Yes

Background/Bio:
Dr. Perrine has a BA in Psychology, a MA in Human Sexuality and a PhD in Clinical Psychology. He garners over ten years experience in the study of human sexuality focusing on the needs and wants of gay men. He devotes precious time and energy to each client and provides insight into building healthy and happy relationships.

Process/Personal Style:
Individuals complete their Private Matchmaking Profile online utilizing the Comprehensive Partner Perfect Compatibility™ System and subscribe for an initial consult. Dr. Perrine, Relationship Expert, provides a one-on-one consultation. After each introduction, a follow-up consultation is conducted. Relationship consulting and coaching are also available.

Pricing/Service: $$$
Includes: Absolutely discreet and confidential services, one-on-one comprehensive needs-and-wants assessment, arranged introductions, follow-up consultations with clients and potential matches, relationship consulting and coaching, quarterly dating analysis, invitations to private mixers and socials.

Credentials: MMI Network Member

Pretty People International
Melodee Ghosn
Established in 1997
Located in Los Angeles, CA 90049
P: 310-471-8002
E: pp2000bh@aol.com

Category: Dating; Relationship; Marriage
Company Motto: Pretty People International – where dreams come true.

At a glance:
- Service: Clients to Clients
- Age range: Male clients: 35–70; female clients: 28–60
- Market focus: Upscale professionals; 50% are Jewish, many are high profile and affluent
- Serving: 1) Los Angeles; 2) Orange County and San Diego and European clients
- Number of Clients (paying): 400
- Pre-screening: Clients: Yes
- Show pictures: Clients: Yes

Background/Bio:
Pretty People International is a discreet and exclusive matchmaking service in Southern California. They specialize in matching successful, attractive, and upscale professionals. In addition, they represent European clients. They do not advertise, have no web site, and most of the clients are by referral.

Process/Personal Style:
They schedule meeting/interview with the potential client. If the client is accepted, they would take a photo or have them provide us with a current photo. The client would see a portfolio of members and choose the ones they would like to meet. If they want to meet each other, numbers are exchanged and they schedule a meeting. Pretty People International also does personal searches. Photos, bios and numbers are exchanged via e-mail.

Pricing/Service: $$$
Includes: One year of unlimited introductions. If the client gets married, there is an additional fee.

Ignite Matchmaking Service
Sheryl Williams
Established in 2006
Located in Arvada, CO 80007
P: 303-929-7304
E: sheryl@ignitematchmaking.com
W: www.ignitematchmaking.com

Category: Dating; Marriage
Company Motto: The Spark Starts Here

At a glance:
- Service: Clients to Clients; Clients to Members
- Age range: Male clients: 30–64; female clients: 24–67
- Market focus: Professionals
- Serving: Denver/Boulder and Front Range, CO
- Number of Clients (paying): 300; Members (non-paying): 1,000
- Pre-Screening: Clients: Yes; Members: Yes
- Show pictures: Clients: Yes; Members: Yes

Background/Bio:
Sheryl Williams began matchmaking 20 years ago and has many clients marriages under her belt. A 30-year resident of Colorado, she's built an extensive network. With a warm, welcoming personality, Sheryl can help you find happiness in the relationship you've been looking for.

Process/Personal Style:
Clients complete an online application followed by an interview. Then Ignite Matchmaking Service searches its database for a match. They present the woman's picture with information to their male clients. If the man is interested, they present the man's picture and information to the woman. If they agree to meet, Ignite arranges the date.

Pricing/Service: $$
Includes:
For Men: searching for a match, arranging the dates, date coaching, follow up.
For Women: matching women with my men, arranging dates, date coaching and follow up, reviewing online profiles if they participate in an online dating service, and much more.

Credentials: **BBB**

Introductions
Dottie Ricketson
Established in 2003
Located in 1400 Larimer Street
Denver, CO 80202
P: 303-530-1933
E: dottie@introusa.com
W: www.introusa.com
Category: Dating; Relationship; Marriage
Company Motto: High-end personalized matchmaking

At a glance:
- Service: Clients to Clients
- Age range: Male clients: 35–75; female clients: 35–75
- Market focus: Affluent professionals
- Serving: Greater Denver and Boulder, CO
- Number of Clients (paying): 200
- Pre-screening: Clients: Yes
- Show pictures: Clients: No

Background/Bio:
Dottie has been a resident of the Denver and Boulder area for over 30 years and brings to Introductions a wealth of experience in helping others. She is fully engaged in helping single men and women find that special someone. A self-professed romantic, Dottie loves helping people by making introductions that often lead to expanded possibilities. With a strong business background, a genuine love of people, and a high energy personality, it's no wonder Dottie Ricketson is one of Colorado's favorite matchmakers. Along the way, Dottie has also been active in many nonprofit charitable organizations, an involvement she continues today by donating Introduction's gift certificates to many charity functions. Additionally, Introductions sponsors singles' charity events to benefit local chapters of national nonprofit organizations and to provide ways for her clients to meet other singles.

Process/Personal Style:
Interview, selection, profile review, receive potential match profile, discuss, set up reservation at restaurant, feedback after each date.

Pricing/Service: $$

It's Just Lunch
Established 1999
Located in Denver, CO 80202
P: 303-292-2600
E: angela@ijlden.com
W: www.it'sjustlunchdenver.com

Category: Dating; Relationship; Marriage
Company Motto: It's Just Lunch, a dating service for busy professionals.

At a glance:
- Service: Clients to Clients
- Market focus: Busy professionals
- Serving: Denver, Colorado
- Number of Clients (paying): 3,500–5,000
- Pre-screening: Clients: Yes
- Show pictures: Clients: No

Background/Bio:
It's Just Lunch was started fifteen years ago for busy professionals to meet in a low-pressure, discreet setting: lunch.

Process/Personal Style:
Confidential personal service: they personally pick all matches, contact their clients by phone to tell them about their match, make the reservation for them. Their clients just show up for lunch and many of their dates turn into second dates.

Pricing/Service: $$

Catherine's Connections
Kate McCabe
Established in 1998
Located in greater Manhattan area
Corporate Office: Stony Creek, CT 06405
P: 212-543-0099; 888-968-5283
E: catherinesconnections@msn.com
W: www.catherinesconnections.com

Category: Dating; Coaching; Relationship; Marriage
Company Motto: Introductions to Mature Mates of Means Over 40™

At a glance:
- Service: Matches Clients to Clients of equal caliber
- Age Range: Male clients: Over 40; female clients: over 40
- Market Focus: Mature Mates of Means over 40—Jewish and Non-Jewish
- Serving: 1) Tri-State (NY, CT, NJ) 2) Boca and Boston
- Number of Clients (paying): 800; Members (non-paying): 50
- Show pictures Clients: No; Members: No

Background/Bio:
Catherine's background: Went to prep school in New York City. Graduated from Skidmore College. Worked in the fashion field for 10 years. Debut Florida. Currently President of Catherine's Connections last 10 years. Member of Garden Club and The Pine Orchard Yacht and Country Club. Married to Colonel Steven Vass.

Process/Personal Style:
Highly personalized introductions to other members of the same status.

Pricing/Service: $$$$

Credentials: Member of Manhattan Chamber of Commerce; MMI Network Member

Great Date Now
Gary Ferone
Located in Milford and Darien, CT
P: 203-877-2500; 203-655-8400
E: gary@greatdatenow.com
W: www.greatdatenow.com

Category: Dating; Coaching; Relationship; Marriage
Company Motto: Personalizes matchmaking for professional, discerning singles

At a glance:
- Service: Clients to Clients; Clients to Members
- Age range: Male clients: 22–75; female clients: 22–70
- Market focus: Professional discerning singles
- Serving: 1) Westchester, Long Island and Manhattan; 2) Bergen, NJ; Fairfield and New Haven, CT
- Number of Clients (paying): 2,000; Members (non-paying): 250
- Pre-screening: Clients: Yes; Members: Yes
- Show pictures: Clients: No; Members: No

Background/Bio:
Tri-state single professionals frequently find themselves frustrated with the process of dating. Great Date Now will help singles find the right relationship by carefully arranging quality dates with singles like them. Privately owned and operated, Great Date Now has developed a new approach to the old-fashioned method of matchmaking. Their clients tell them about the type of person they are looking for and let them do the rest. With personalization and intuition, combined with an outstanding list of single professionals, they will work toward finding the right match for their client.

Process/Personal Style:
Their goal is to remove the discouragement and time consuming efforts so often met with while trying to find that special someone. The bar scene, work environment encounters, and Internet dating can be awkward, disappointing, and depressing. They feel that the personalization in the matchmaking process brings dignity to dating.

Pricing/Service: $$ to $$$

Credentials: MMI Network Member

VIP Life
Lisa Clampitt, CSW, CMM
Established in 2000
Located in New York, NY 10003
P: 212-242-4755
E: lisa@clubviplife.com
W: www.clubviplife.com

Category: Coaching; Relationship; Marriage
Company Motto: An Elite Social Club

At a glance:
- Service: Clients to Members
- Age range: Male clients: 25–65; female members: 21–45
- Market focus: Professional introductions of successful male clients to exceptional, relationship-oriented female members.
- Serving: 1) Connecticut; 2) New York, New Jersey
- Number of Clients (paying): 20; Members (non-paying): 1,000
- Pre-screening: Clients: Yes; Members: Yes
- Show pictures: Clients: Yes; Members: No

Background/Bio:
Lisa Clampitt, CSW, is the founder and president of VIP Life, a professional match-maker and relationship expert since the late 90s and a New York State Certified Social Worker since 1991. Lisa is a natural born matchmaker who constantly introduced her friends to people she felt would be best suited for them, which resulted in many marriages and dozens of children. She has taken her hands-on personal approach and applied her techniques and passion to her professional life of matchmaking.

Process/Personal Style:
A one-on-one personal interview assesses your relationship goals and objective. Male clients review pictures and profiles of female members to assess if this service is right for him. If he decides to join, he receives unlimited introductions to appropriate female members. After each date, feedback is given to assess what worked and what didn't.

Pricing/Service: $$$ to $$$$$
Includes: Unlimited introductions, date and relationship feedback and coaching, concierge services.

Credentials: Certified Matchmaker and Certified Social Worker MMI Network Member Member of the Board of Directors of the Professional and Certified Matchmakers Network.

Distinctive Search, Inc.
Teresa Ann Foxworthy
Established in 1996
Located in Washington, DC
P: 888-800-1241
E: info@originaldatingcoach.com
W: www.matchmakercoach.com & www.originaldatingcoach.com

Category: Dating; Coaching; Relationship; Marriage
Company Motto: Attract and keep the love of your life!

At a glance:
- Service: Clients to Members
- Age range: Male clients: 25+; female clients: 25+
- Market focus: Marriage-oriented professionals
- Serving: 1) San Francisco Bay Area/San Diego Area; 2) Baltimore, Washington
- Number of Clients (paying): 10; Members (non-paying): 3,500+
- Pre-screening: Clients: Yes; Members: Yes
- Show pictures: Clients: Yes; Members: Yes

Background/Bio:
Teresa Ann Foxworthy founded Love in the 21st Century to offer distinctive search matchmaking introductions and original dating coaching programs for professionals ready to meet and keep the love of their life! Her background includes a counseling practice of 17 years, life coaching for over 10, and pioneering in the field of personal transformation for over 20 years.

Process/Personal Style:
Ms. Foxworthy's clients are invited to a complimentary 30-minute consultation to get acquainted with her and her programs. Matchmaking clients are delighted by her caring yet savvy approach to get results fast. Her first objective is seeing how ready clients are for dating or marriage and then understanding what kind of person would be the best match for them.

Pricing/Service: $$$ to $$$$
Includes: 6 introductions in 6 months; 12 introductions in 12 months; 2-hour orientation consultation; and much, much more.

Credentials: MMI Network Member

Elite Love Registry, LLC
Kailen Rosenberg
Established in 2006
Located in Washington, DC
P: 877-930-5683
E: kailenluv@aol.com
W: www.eliteloveregistry.com

Category: Dating; Coaching; Relationship; Marriage
Company Motto: Where healthy relationships begin.

At a glance:
- Service: Clients to Clients; Clients to Members; Clients to Subscribers
- Age range: Male and female clients: late 20s to mid 70s
- Market focus: all, yet elite and healthy-minded "most eligible in the country"
- Serving: 1) Atlanta; 2) Chicago, Minnesota, Dallas, Las Vegas, New York, Seattle, Cincinnati, Denver, Los Angeles, Scottsdale, Washington, DC, and international locatons
- Number of Clients (paying): hundreds; Members (non-paying): thousands
- Pre-screening: Clients: Yes; Members: Yes
- Show pictures: Clients: Yes; Members: No

Background/Bio:
Kailen Rosenberg is a nationally recognized and sought after relationship expert and life designer to the elite. Over 15 years ago, Kailen designed a methodology based on certain principles, proven to create true elegance and success in the personal lives of healthy-minded, busy, successful individuals around the globe. She is a respected in-novator in her field and is celebrity endorsed and supported by nationally acclaimed experts. Kailen has been recognized for "doing it ethically" by the *Seattle Times*.

Process/Personal Style:
Their members are highly pre-screened and background checked. To provide a safe and secure experience for their members, all potential members must pass a three-step screening process, and are only selected after a personal face-to-face interview has oc-curred.

Pricing/Service: $ to $$$$
Includes: A phone interview, a face-to-face assessment, an extensive background and identity check, love and self-image blue prints with a personal love architect™

My Partner Perfect
Dr. Patrick Perrine
Established in 2004
Located in: San Francisco, CA 94101
P: 415-358-6868; 877-225-5928
E: matchmaking@mypartnerperfect.com
W: www.mypartnerperfect.com

Category: Dating; Coaching; Relationship; Partnerships
Company Motto: Not everything in life is temporary

At a glance:
- Service: Clients to Members
- Age range: Male clients: 25–75
- Market focus: gay men
- Serving: Clients nationally
- Number of Clients (paying): No more than 30 at a time; Members (non-paying): Thousands
- Pre-screening: Clients: Yes; Members: Yes
- Show pictures: Clients: Yes; Members: Yes

Background/Bio:
Dr. Perrine has a BA in Psychology, a MA in Human Sexuality and a PhD in Clinical Psychology. He garners over ten years experience in the study of human sexuality focusing on the needs and wants of gay men. He devotes precious time and energy to each client and provides insight into building healthy and happy relationships.

Process/Personal Style:
Individuals complete their Private Matchmaking Profile online utilizing the Comprehensive Partner Perfect Compatibility™ System and subscribe for an initial consult. Dr. Patrick Perrine, Relationship Expert, provides a one-on-one consultation. After each introduction, a follow-up consultation is conducted. Relationship consulting and coaching are also available.

Pricing/Service: $$$
Includes: Absolutely discreet and confidential services, personalized intake and matchmaking, one-on-one comprehensive needs-and-wants assessment, arranged introductions, follow-up consultations with clients and potential matches, relationship consulting and coaching, quarterly dating analysis, invitations to private mixers and socials.

Credentials: MMI Network Member

Catherine's Connections
Kate McCabe
Established in 1998
Located in Boca Raton, FL
P: 888-968-5283
E: catherinesconnections@msn.com
W: www.catherinesconnections.com

Category: Dating; Coaching; Relationship; Marriage
Company Motto: Introductions to Mature Mates of Means Over 40™

At a glance:
• Service: Matches Clients to Clients of equal caliber
• Age Range: Male clients: over 40; female clients: over 40
• Market Focus: Mature Mates of Means and over 40—Jewish and Non-Jewish
• Serving: 1) Tri-State (NY, CT, NJ) 2) Boca and Boston
• Number of Clients (paying): 800; Members (non-paying): 50
• Show pictures: Clients: No; Members: No

Background/Bio:
Catherine's background: Went to prep school in New York City. Graduated from Skidmore College. Worked in the fashion field for 10 years. Debut Florida. Currently President of Catherine's Connections last 10 years. Member of Garden Club and The Pine Orchard Yacht and Country Club. Married to Colonel Steven Vass.

Process/Personal Style:
Highly personalized introductions to other members of the same status.

Pricing/Service: $$$$

Credentials: Member of Manhattan Chamber of Commerce; MMI Network Member

Elite Introductions
Elisabeth Dabbelt
Established in 1987
Located in Altamont Springs, FL 32701
P: 407-671-8300
E: elisabeth@elitesingleprofessionals.com
W: www.orlandosingleprofessionals.com

Category: Dating; Coaching; Relationship; Marriage
Company Motto: Elite creates relationships

At a glance:
- Service: Clients to Clients
- Age range: Male clients: 32–82; female clients: 26–85
- Serving: All of central Florida
- Number of Clients (paying): All
- Pre-screening: Clients: Yes

Background/Bio:
Orlando's most experienced and professional matchmaker, Elisabeth Dabbelt understands that the more you have to offer, the more difficult it is to find that special partner. She takes a personal interest in your very special and unique requirements. Elite Introductions was founded to provide a safe, effective, and dignified alternative for finding your appropriate life partner.

Process/Personal Style:
Elite Introductions considers social and economic backgrounds, values, and interests, as well as other specific considerations provided by each client necessary for a successful match. All introductions will be approved by you in advance, so there are no blind dates. You will be provided with important information in the profile of each potential candidate. You choose whom you want to meet based on recommended guidance and suggestions. The entire process is discreet, safe, dignified, and most of all, results oriented.

Pricing/Service: $$$
Includes: Private introductions. Mutual agreement of two people desiring to meet.

Credentials: BBB

Kelleher & Associates Inc
Amber Kelleher
Established in 1986
Located in West Palm Beach, FL
P: 800-401-MATCH (6282)
E: info@kelleher-associates.com
W: www.meettheelite.com

Category: Dating; Coaching; Relationship; Marriage
Company Motto: Exquisite matchmaking since 1986.

At a glance:
- Service: Clients to Clients; Clients to Members
- Age range: Male clients: 25 and up; female clients: 25 and up
- Market focus: Busy professionals and affluent entrepreneurs nationwide
- Serving: 1) Scottsdale; 2) California, Chicago, West Palm Beach, Dallas, Las Vegas, and New York
- Pre-screening: Clients: Yes; Members: Yes
- Show pictures: Clients: Yes; Members: No

Background/Bio:
The ultra-exclusive mother–daughter matchmaking team of Kelleher & Associates was founded by Jill Kelleher in 1986. Kelleher & Associates caters to an exceptional clientele. Noted as a National Search Firm, we represent the best and brightest in the U.S. as well as abroad. We are distinguished by our stellar reputation, priority on discretion, and a proprietary database, resulting from over two decades in our industry. Boasting a staff of over 30 full-time matchmakers nationwide with domestic offices that include New York, San Francisco, Beverly Hills, Scottsdale, La Jolla, West Palm Beach, Dallas, Las Vegas, Chicago, and Silicon Valley.

Process/Personal Style:
Once an applicant is successfully accepted, Kelleher clients are provided with a very unique, personalized service like no other. Each of their introductions are hand-selected with great detail and are based on their client's specific criteria. Kelleher & Associates set the standard for matchmaking over 20 years ago, and continues to do so today.

Pricing/Service: $$$$ to $$$$$
Includes: One full year of quality introductions, with additional year of hold extensions. Custom memberships may also include relationship experts, psychiatrists, and life coaches.

Credentials: **BBB**

112

Options
Steve & Naomi
Established in 1994
Located in Atlanta, GA 30309
P: 800-360-3283
E: rp@optionsdate.com
W: www.optionsdate.com & www.gayoptions.com

Category: Dating; Relationship; Marriage
Company Motto: Personalized matchmaking for those seeking quality relationships.

At a glance:
- Service: Clients to Clients
- Age range: Male clients: 21–80s; female clients: 21–80s
- Market focus: professionals; self-employed; heterosexuals; gays and lesbians
- Serving: 1) South Florida; 2) Los Angeles, CA; VA, DC, MD, DE, PA, NJ, NYC, Long Island, Lower CT, GA, and AL
- Number of Clients (paying): 11,000+
- Pre-screening: Clients: Yes
- Show pictures: Clients: No

Background/Bio:
The two owners have over 35 years of combined experience in the dating industry. Steve has a Masters in aerospace engineering and handles the back end of the business while Naomi has been passionately matching since 1983. The couple met in 1997, got married, and have been jointly running Options dating service ever since.

Process/Personal Style:
A personalized offline dating service with matches based on compatibility and physical qualities. All applicants are screened in person with all vital information and personal statistics guaranteed. All new applicants must undergo a background check.

Pricing/Service: $$ to $$$

Credentials: **BBB**

113

Traditional Matchmakers
Beatrice Gruss, PhD
Established in 1983
Located in Atlanta, GA 30327
P: 404-237-8593
E: beatrice@traditionalmatchmakers.com
W: www.traditionalmatchmakers.com

Category: Dating; Relationship; Marriage
Company Motto: Our priority is to cultivate and maintain a pool of clients of the highest caliber.

At a glance:
- Service: Clients to Clients
- Age range: Male clients: 28–70; female clients: 25–60
- Market focus: Professionals
- Serving: Atlanta, GA
- Number of Clients (paying): about 400
- Pre-screening: Clients: Yes
- Show pictures: Clients: Yes

Background/Bio:
Beatrice Gruss was born in Bucharest, Romania, and grew up in Paris and Mexico City. She holds a BA in literature from Berkeley and an MA from New York University, as well as her PhD course work in French and Spanish literature from Emory University. She speaks five languages and used to teach before becoming a matchmaker. She founded Traditional Matchmakers in 1983. Beatrice lives in Atlanta, Georgia, with her husband Benson Caplan. Between them they have five children and five grandchildren thus far.

Process/Personal Style:
Meeting someone of their same caliber without being exposed to the vagaries of the Internet.

Pricing/Service: $

Credentials: **BBB**

 **Kelleher & Associates, Inc.**
Amber Kelleher
Established in 1986
Located in Chicago, IL
P: 800-401-MATCH (6282)
E: info@kelleher-associates.com
W: www.meettheelite.com

Category: Dating; Coaching; Relationship; Marriage
Company Motto: Exquisite matchmaking since 1986.

At a glance:
- Service: Clients to Clients; Clients to Members
- Age range: Male clients: 25 and up; female clients: 25 and up
- Market focus: Busy professionals and affluent entrepreneurs nationwide
- Serving: 1) Scottsdale; 2) California, Chicago, West Palm Beach, Dallas, Las Vegas, and New York
- Pre-screening: Clients: Yes; Members: Yes
- Show pictures: Clients: Yes; Members: No

Background/Bio:
The ultra-exclusive mother–daughter matchmaking team of Kelleher & Associates was founded by Jill Kelleher in 1986. Kelleher & Associates caters to an exceptional clientele. Noted as a National Search Firm, we represent the best and brightest in the U.S. as well as abroad. We are distinguished by our stellar reputation, priority on discretion, and a proprietary database, resulting from over two decades in our industry. Boasting a staff of over 30 full-time matchmakers nationwide with domestic offices that include New York, San Francisco, Beverly Hills, Scottsdale, La Jolla, West Palm Beach, Dallas, Las Vegas, Chicago, and Silicon Valley.

Process/Personal Style:
Once an applicant is successfully accepted, Kelleher clients are provided with a very unique, personalized service like no other. Each of their introductions are hand-selected with great detail and are based on their client's specific criteria. Kelleher & Associates set the standard for matchmaking over 20 years ago, and continues to do so today.

Pricing/Service: $$$$ to $$$$$
Includes: One full year of quality introductions, with additional year of hold extensions. Custom memberships may also include relationship experts, psychiatrists, and life coaches.

Credentials: **BBB**

115

Selective Search Inc.
Barbie Adler
Established in 2000
Located in Chicago, IL
P: 866-592-1200
E: barbie@selectivesearch-inc.com
W: www.selectivesearch-inc.com

Category: Coaching; Relationship; Marriage
Company Motto: Elite matchmakers to the most eligible, commitment-minded bachelors.

At a glance:
- Service: Clients to Members
- Market focus: affluent professionals
- Serving: 1) Phoenix, AZ; 2) Chicago, New York, Los Angeles, Orange County, San Francisco, Atlanta, Dallas, Miami, Washington, DC, St. Louis
- Number of Clients (paying): 100; Members (non-paying): 50,000
- Pre-Screening: Clients: Yes; Members: Yes
- Show pictures: Clients: Yes; Members: upon request

Background/Bio:
Barbie Adler, founder and president of Selective Search, one the leading off-line personal matchmaking firms with clients across the country, is one of the industry's most respected matchmakers, soughtafter lifestyle management coach and personal relationship expert. Profiled as an authority on relationships by *Forbes, Fortune, The Economist, The Wall Street Journal, USA Today, Self magazine, Men's Heath,* and CNN, among others, Barbie's expertise in the matchmaking world is in high demand.

Process/Personal Style:
Exclusive within the industry, Selective Search represents a new paradigm in matchmaking, that of the "executive recruiter." The approach, the process, and the results are unique to Selective Search and are a testament to Barbie's vision of helping individuals find each other in a very personal, yet effective and efficient environment.

Pricing/Service: $$$$$
Includes: One year membership, ten introductions

Credentials: MMI Network Member

Matchmaker International
Mary Ann
Located in Fort Wayne, IN 46845
P: 260-637-4300
W: www.matchmakerinternational.com

Category: Dating; Relationship
Company Motto: Intelligent solutions for selective people.

At a glance:
- Service: Clients to Clients
- Age range: Male clients: 21+; female clients: 21+
- Market focus: Professional heterosexuals
- Serving: 1) Indiana; 2) Ohio; Michigan
- Number of Clients (paying): All
- Pre-screening: Clients: Yes
- Show pictures: Clients: No

Background/Bio:
Match together men and women with no criminal violations and no mental problems. We look for high quality, positive, honest people with good values and high morals.

Process/Personal Style:
We match on physical appearance, compatibility, and we suggest 5 years + or -.

Pricing/Service: $$
Includes: 8 introductions

Credentials:

Compatible Connections, LLC
Elaine Michaels
Established in 2001
Located in Cedar Rapids, IA
P: 319-377-0040
E: connect@compatible-connections.com
W: www.compatible-connections.com

Category: Dating; Coaching; Relationship, Marriage
Company Motto: Helping You Become Two

At a glance:
- Service: Clients to Clients
- Age range: Male clients: 18–80; female clients: 18–80
- Market focus: everyone is considered
- Serving: Eastern Iowa
- Number of clients (paying): 250
- Pre-screening: Clients: Yes
- Show pictures: Clients: No

Background/Bio:
Elaine Michaels is president of Compatible Connections, a privately held Introduction Service for busy singles. Ms. Michaels has been self-employed for more than 25 years, owning and operating two very successful businesses. An experienced single herself, Elaine saw first-hand how difficult it was to meet others. In her journey she had met many singles who echoed the same sentiments, and, as a result, founded Compatible Connections nearly six years ago.

Process/Style:
A client meets with Elaine and can choose from ten memberships. The one chosen dictates how their membership will work and with what benefits. The client fills out a profile, photos are taken, and then the process of searching (done by the client or Elaine) for a match begins. When two clients mutually want to meet they are introduced personally by Elaine. The ultimate Personal Matchmaker membership allows Elaine to hand-select potential matches from the community for her special clients.

Pricing/Service: $ to $$$
Includes: Personally meeting with clients, profile completed by client, photos taken, various benefits including time-out, coaching, advice/feedback, and makeover/image consulting; assistance and introductions done personally by Elaine.

Perfect Mate
Anne Teachworth, CMM
Established in 2006
Located in Metairie/New Orleans, Louisiana 70005
P: 504-828-2072 and 888-828-MATE
E: ateachw@aol.com, teach@perfectmateinc.com
W: www.annethematchmaker.com, www.innercouple.com

Category: Coaching; Relationship; Marriage
Company Motto: Learn the important difference between a Perfect Mate and a Perfect Match.

At a glance:
* Service: Clients to Members
* Age range: Male clients: 40–90; female clients: 40–90
* Market focus: All singles (widowed, separated, or divorced) who want to be married.
* Serving: New Orleans and suburb of Metairie, and surrounding areas
* Number of Clients (paying): 16; Members (non-paying): 20
* Pre-screening: Clients: Yes; Members: Yes
* Show pictures: Clients: Yes; Members: No

Background/Bio:
I am a counselor with 30 years experience in the field, specializing in couples, pre-marital, marriage, parenting, and family counseling. I am the author of a book, *Why We Pick The Mates We Do*, available on Amazon.com, and the developer of The Psychogenetic System of mate selection, which I teach to therapists at conferences all over the world. I have offices in both New Orleans and New York, with representatives in San Francisco, Seattle, Chicago, and Washington, DC.

Process/Personal Style:
The first Interview with Anne or J. B. includes childhood and relationship history, two psychological tests. The second interview consists of test results and recommendations. You can then choose to enroll as a Preferred Single, which puts you on our list to meet one of our clients.

Pricing/Service: $$
Includes: Psychological testing, feedback, coaching, dinner parties, classes

Credentials:

119

The Matchmaker
Ron
Established in 1997
Located in Portland Maine 04101
P: 207-775-2288
E: matchmakerofmaine@yahoo.com
W: www.matchmakerofmaine.com

Category: Dating; Relationship; Marriage
Company Motto: Dating made easy.

At a glance:
- Service: Clients to Clients
- Age range: Male clients: 27–77; female clients: 24–69
- Market focus: Professionals
- Serving: 1) Maine; 2) New Hampshire
- Number of Clients (paying): 450
- Pre-screening: Clients: Yes
- Show pictures: Clients: Yes

Process/Personal Style:
1) One hour free consultation; one half-hour at-home completing personality profile application
2) Background check done on all new members.
3) Personal matchmaking done for each client.
4) Client can review and see photos and profiles of other members that fit their requirements.
5) Feedback required after meeting takes place.

Pricing/Service: $

Credentials: BBB

Distinctive Search, Inc.
Teresa Ann Foxworthy
Established in 1996
Located in Baltimore, MD
P: 888-800-1241
E: info@originaldatingcoach.com
W: www.matchmakercoach.com & www.originaldatingcoach.com

Category: Dating; Coaching; Relationship; Marriage
Company Motto: Attract and keep the love of your life!

At a glance:
- Service: Clients to Members
- Age range: Male clients: 25+; female clients: 25+
- Market focus: Marriage-oriented professionals
- Serving: 1) San Francisco Bay area/San Diego area; 2) Baltimore, Washington
- Number of Clients (paying): 10; Members (non-paying): 3,500+
- Pre-screening: Clients: Yes; Members: Yes
- Show pictures: Clients: Yes; Members: Yes

Background/Bio:
Teresa Ann Foxworthy founded Love in the 21st Century to offer distinctive search matchmaking introductions and original dating coaching programs for professionals ready to meet and keep the love of their life! Her background includes a counseling practice of 17 years, life coaching for over 10, and pioneering in the field of personal transformation for over 20 years.

Process/Personal Style:
Ms. Foxworthy's clients are invited to a complimentary 30-minute consultation to get acquainted with her and her programs. Matchmaking clients are delighted by her caring yet savvy approach to getting results fast. Her first objective is seeing how ready clients are for dating or marriage and then understanding what kind of person would be the best match for them.

Pricing/Service: $$$ to $$$$
Includes: 6 introductions in 6 months; 12 introductions in 12 months; 2-hour orientation consultation; and much, much more.

Credentials: MMI Network Member

Leora Hoffman Associates
Leora Hoffman, Practicing Attorney
Established in 1989
Located in Bethesda, MD 20827
P: 301-537-5266

E: leora@leorahoffman.com
W: www.leorahoffman.com

Category: Dating; Coaching; Relationship; Marriage
Company Motto: When it comes to relationships, there's no substitute for the personal touch.

At a glance:
- Service: Clients to Clients; Clients to Members
- Age range: Male clients: 32–70; female clients: 30–70
- Market focus: Jewish professional singles (75% of my population)
- Serving: 1) Baltimore, MD; 2) Washington, DC area
- Number of Clients (paying): 100; Members (non-paying): 400
- Pre-screening: Clients: Yes; Members: Yes
- Show pictures: Clients: No; Members: No

Background/Bio:
Ms. Hoffman founded her business for busy Washington, DC–area professionals, after taking a hiatus from the practice of law in 1989. She has had 63 marriages to her credit over the years, as well as hundreds of relationships, and takes pride in her advocacy skills, which make her an effective matchmaker. Leora appeared on cable TV, has written an advice column for singles, and continues to speak publicly to singles groups on various issues involving singles in the local community.

Process/Personal Style:
Leora Hoffman Associates offers a comprehensive initial consultation which includes a complete family, work, and relationship history on the client. Once a client joins, they work closely with them as a coach/advocate to offer referrals, field feedback, and make appropriate recommendations until the client's goal is met.

Pricing/Service: $ to $$$$
Includes: Referrals, feedback from dates, relationship advice/coaching.

Credentials: **BBB**

Catherine's Connections
Kate McCabe
Established in 1998
Located in Boston, MA
Corporate Office: Stony Creek, CT 06405
P: 888-968-5283
E: catherinesconnections@msn.com
W: www.catherinesconnections.com

Category: Dating; Coaching; Relationship; Marriage
Company Motto: Introductions to Mature Mates of Means Over 40™

At a glance:
- Service: Matches Clients to Clients of equal caliber
- Age Range: Male clients: Over 40; female clients: over 40
- Market Focus: Mature Mates of Means and over 40—Jewish and Non-Jewish
- Serving: 1) Tri-State (NY, CT, NJ); 2) Boca and Boston
- Number of Clients (paying): 800; Members (non-paying): 50
- Show pictures: Clients: No; Members: No

Background/Bio:
Catherine's background: Went to prep school in New York City. Graduated from Skidmore College. Worked in the fashion field for 10 years. Debut Florida. Currently President of Catherine's Connections last 10 years. Member of Garden Club and The Pine Orchard Yacht and Country Club. Married to Colonel Steven Vass.

Process/Personal Style:
Highly personalized introductions to other members of the same status.

Pricing/Service: $$$$

Credentials: Member of Manhattan Chamber of Commerce; MMI Network Member

Matchmaker International
Christy Tromp, CMM
Established in 1989
Located in Grand Rapids, MI
P: 616-827-1700
E: matchmakerintl@sbcglobal.net
W: www.matchmakermichigan.com

Category: Dating; Coaching; Relationship; Marriage
Company Motto: The right one is out there for everyone!

At a glance:
- Service: Clients to Clients
- Age range: Male clients: 18–99; female clients: 18–99
- Market focus: Singles, aged 18–99
- Serving: 1) Grand Rapids; 2) Flint and Troy Michigan
- Number of Clients (paying): 3,000+
- Pre-screening: Clients: Yes
- Show pictures: Clients: No

Background/Bio:
Besides being a certified matchmaker, Christy is also a certified spa therapist and image consultant. It is her goal that her clients feel their best, look their best, and find success.

Process/Personal Style:
Christy meets with her clients in person. She develops a complete background check on her clients and a profile on the person they are looking to meet. She has a private investigator, through the service, who does a complete background check on everyone. She also has a beautiful spa therapy center and a wonderful massage therapist, exclusively for her clients. She makes the whole process as fun and relaxing as possible.

Pricing/Service: $$ to $$$

Credentials: MMI Network Member

Global Love Mergers
Kailen Rosenberg
Established in 2001
Located in Mimetonka, MN
P: 877-930-5683
E: kailenluv@aol.com
W: www.globallovemergers.com

Category: Dating; Coaching; Relationship; Marriage
Company Motto: Where healthy relationships begin.

At a glance:

- Service: Clients to Clients; Clients to Members; Clients to Subscribers
- Age range: Male and female clients: late 20s to mid 70s
- Market focus: Elite and healthy-minded individuals.
- Serving: 1) Minnesota; 2) nationally and internationally
- Number of Clients (paying): hundreds; Members (non-paying): thousands
- Pre-screening: Clients: Yes; Members: Yes
- Show pictures: Clients: Yes; Members: No

Background/Bio:
Kailen Rosenberg has over 15 years experience and knowledge in the dating service industry. She has an incredible passion for helping people achieve success both personally and professionally. She is a highly successful love and self-image designer who is extremely intuitive when it comes to helping people find their own inner and outer beauty. Kailen has introduced hundreds of successful singles into wonderful relationships and has succeeded in introducing over 100 marriages.

Process/Personal Style:
Each client is thoroughly prescreened, interviewed, subject to a reference check, and completes a Home Visit. They also go through several hours of preparation with Kailen Rosenberg personally to ensure their readiness for meeting their potential soul mate.

Pricing/Service: $$$ to $$$$$
Includes: A truly unique high-end, one-on-one service between you and Kailen. It consists of the initial interview, the Self-Image and Relationship Readiness Assessment and coaching, the Home Visit, on-going personal time and attention, a specially-designed search for your soul mate, and contact and feedback throughout the process.

Credentials: **BBB**

Preference Introductions
Rhonda Davidson
Established in 1982
Located in Springfield, MO
P: 417-881-1230
E: rhonda@qualitysingles.info
W: www.todayssingles.com

Category: Dating; Coaching; Relationship; Marriage
Company Motto: Private, sincere, quality singles...because there's someone for everyone!

At a glance:
• Service: Clients to Clients
• Age range: Male clients: 21–80; female clients: 21–80
• Market focus: Professional, quality singles
• Serving: Southwest Missouri including Springfield, Joplin, Branson, Lebanon
• Pre-screening: Clients: Yes
• Show pictures: Clients: No

Background/Bio:
Rhonda Davidson became single at age 38. She tried everything most people do to try to meet quality singles, including church, internet dating as well as bars, all of which were unsuccessful. A highly respected businesswoman suggested she try a local reputable dating service. Rhonda joined Preference in February 2002 and loved the experience and concept so much that she became the owner by June. She is now in her fifth year and on her third expansion. She truly has a passion for matchmaking and continues to spread love throughout southwest Missouri!

Process/Personal Style:
First step is to set up a private consultation. All applicants are required to consent to a nationwide background check. The company's focus is to match quality singles with other quality singles with many levels of compatibility such as common interests, goals ,and values. They don't rely on computers to select matches, they hand select them personally, according to their "preferences." They have represented thousands of singles of all different walks of life. They are not concerned about how much money someone has but rather if they live a quality life and are sincere.

Pricing/Service: $$

Selective Search, Inc.
Barbie Adler
Established in 2000
Located in St. Louis, MO
P: 866-592-1200
E: barbie@selectivesearch-inc.com
W: www.selectivesearch-inc.com

Category: Coaching; Relationship; Marriage
Company Motto: Elite matchmakers to the most eligible, commitment-minded bachelors.

At a glance:
- Service: Clients to Members
- Market focus: affluent professionals
- Serving: 1) Phoenix, AZ; 2) Chicago, New York, Los Angeles, Orange County, San Francisco, Atlanta, Dallas, Miami, Washington, DC, St. Louis
- Number of Clients (paying): 100; Members (non-paying): 50,000
- Pre-screening: Clients: Yes; Members: Yes
- Show pictures: Clients: Yes; Members: upon request

Background/Bio:
Barbie Adler, founder and president of Selective Search, one the leading off-line personal matchmaking firms with clients across the country, is one of the industry's most respected matchmakers, soughtafter lifestyle management coach and personal relationship expert. Profiled as an authority on relationships by *Forbes, Fortune, The Economist, The Wall Street Journal, USA Today, Self, Men's Heath,* and CNN, among others, Barbie's expertise in the matchmaking world is in high demand.

Process/Personal Style:
Exclusive within the industry, Selective Search represents a new paradigm in matchmaking, that of the "executive recruiter." The approach, the process, and the results are unique to Selective Search and are a testament to Barbie's vision of helping individuals find each other in a very personal, yet effective and efficient environment.

Pricing/Service: $$$$$
Includes: One year membership, ten introductions

Credentials: MMI Network Member **BBB**

Elite Love Registry, LLC
Kailen Rosenberg
Established in 2006
Located in Las Vegas, NV
P: 877-930-5683
E: kailenluv@aol.com
W: www.eliteloveregistry.com

Category: Dating; Coaching; Relationship; Marriage
Company Motto: Where healthy relationships begin.

At a glance:
- Service: Clients to Clients; Clients to Members; Clients to Subscribers
- Age range: Male and female clients: late 20s to mid 70s
- Market focus: all, yet elite and healthy-minded "most eligible in the country"
- Serving: 1) Atlanta; 2) Chicago, Minnesota, Dallas, Las Vegas, New York, Seattle, Cincinnati, Denver, Los Angeles, Scottsdale, Washington, DC, and international locatons
- Number of Clients (paying): hundreds; Members (non-paying): thousands
- Pre-screening: Clients: Yes; Members: Yes
- Show pictures: Clients: Yes; Members: No

Background/Bio:
Kailen Rosenberg is a nationally recognized and sought after relationship expert and life designer to the elite. Over 15 years ago, Kailen designed a methodology based on certain principles, proven to create true elegance and success in the personal lives of healthy-minded, busy, successful individuals around the globe. She is a respected innovator in her field and is celebrity endorsed and supported by nationally acclaimed experts. Kailen has been recognized for "doing it ethically" by the *Seattle Times*.

Process/Personal Style:
Their members are highly pre-screened and background checked. To provide a safe and secure experience for their members, all potential members must pass a three-step screening process, and are only selected after a personal face-to-face interview has occurred.

Pricing/Service: $ to $$$$
Includes: A phone interview, a face-to-face assessment, an extensive background and identity check, love and self-image blue prints with a personal love architect™.

Kelleher & Associates, Inc
Amber Kelleher
Established in 1986
Located in Las Vegas, NV
P: 800-401-MATCH (6282)
E: info@kelleher-associates.com
W: www.meettheelite.com

Category: Dating; Coaching; Relationship; Marriage
Company Motto: Exquisite matchmaking since 1986.

At a glance:
- Service: Clients to Clients; Clients to Members
- Age range: Male clients: 25 and up; female clients: 25 and up
- Market focus: Busy professionals and affluent entrepreneurs nationwide
- Serving: 1) Scottsdale; 2) California, Chicago, West Palm Beach, Dallas, Las Vegas, and New York
- Pre-screening: Clients: Yes; Members: Yes
- Show pictures: Clients: Yes; Members: No

Background/Bio:
The ultra-exclusive mother–daughter matchmaking team of Kelleher & Associates was founded by Jill Kelleher in 1986. Kelleher & Associates caters to an exceptional clientele. Noted as a National Search Firm, we represent the best and brightest in the U.S. as well as abroad. We are distinguished by our stellar reputation, priority on discretion, and a proprietary database, resulting from over two decades in our industry. Boasting a staff of over 30 full-time matchmakers nationwide with domestic offices that include New York, San Francisco, Beverly Hills, Scottsdale, La Jolla, West Palm Beach, Dallas, Las Vegas, Chicago, and Silicon Valley.

Process/Personal Style:
Once an applicant is successfully accepted, Kelleher clients are provided with a very unique, personalized service like no other. Each of their introductions are hand-selected with great detail and are based on their client's specific criteria. Kelleher & Associates set the standard for matchmaking over 20 years ago, and continues to do so today.

Pricing/Service: $$$$ to $$$$$
Includes: One full year of quality introductions, with additional year of hold extensions. Custom memberships may also include relationship experts, psychiatrists, and life coaches.

Credentials: **BBB**

The Matchmaker
Ron
Established in 1997
Located in Portland, ME 04101
P: 207-775-2288
E: matchmakerofmaine@yahoo.com
W: www.matchmakerofmaine.com

Category: Dating; Relationship; Marriage
Company Motto: Dating made easy.

At a glance:
- Service: Clients to Clients
- Age range: Male clients: 27–77; female clients: 24–69
- Market focus: Professionals
- Serving: 1) Maine; 2) New Hampshire
- Number of Clients (paying): 450
- Pre-screening: Clients: Yes
- Show pictures: Clients: Yes

Process/Personal Style:
1) One hour free consultation; one half-hour at-home completing personality profile application
2) Background check done on all new members.
3) Personal matchmaking done for each client.
4) Client can review and see photos and profiles of other members that fit their requirements.
5) Feedback required after meeting takes place.

Pricing/Service: $

Credentials: **BBB**

Together of New Hampshire
Fred Sullivan, Jr.
Established in 1982
Located in Hookser, NH
P: 800-688-5644
E: togethernh@msn.com
W: www.togethernh.com

Category: Dating; Coaching; Relationship; Marriage
Company Motto: Let us introduce you.

At a glance:
- Service: Clients to Clients
- Market focus: Singles generally 30+, divorced, widowed
- Serving: 1) Southern Maine; 2) New Hampshire
- Number of Clients (paying): thousands
- Pre-screening: Clients: Yes
- Show pictures: Clients: Yes

Background/Bio:
Fred Sullivan Jr., president, opened Together's first New Hampshire office in 1982. In 2002, Fred was awarded the Loving Cup Award by Together Corporate Offices for being the longest-running Together franchise owner. Janis Lewis, vice president, came to work at Together in 1987, where she met her husband. She has also married off many friends and a cousin through Together. After managing the business for several years, Janis became part owner with Fred back in 2000.

Process/Personal Style:
A client should expect to start meeting new members within 2–5 weeks of enrolling.

Pricing/Service: $
Includes: Constant support available throughout membership.

Credentials: **BBB**

Catherine's Connections
Kate McCabe
Established in 1998
Located in greater Manhattan area
Corporate Office: Stony Creek, CT 06405
P: 212-543-0099; 888-968-5283
E: catherinesconnections@msn.com
W: www.catherinesconnections.com

Category: Dating; Coaching; Relationship; Marriage
Company Motto: Introductions to Mature Mates of Means Over 40™

At a glance:
- Service: Matches Clients to Clients of equal caliber
- Age Range: Male clients: Over 40; female clients: over 40
- Market Focus: Mature Mates of Means and over 40—Jewish and Non-Jewish
- Serving: 1) Tri-State (NY, CT, NJ) 2) Boca and Boston
- Number of Clients (paying): 800; Members (non-paying): 50
- Show pictures: Clients: No; Members: No

Background/Bio:
Catherine's background: Went to prep school in New York City. Graduated from Skidmore College. Worked in the fashion field for 10 years. Debut Florida. Currently President of Catherine's Connections last 10 years. Member of Garden Club and The Pine Orchard Yacht and Country Club. Married to Colonel Steven Vass.

Process/Personal Style:
Highly personalized introductions to other members of the same status.

Pricing/Service: $$$$ (programs vary)

Credentials: Member of Manhattan Chamber of Commerce; MMI Network Member

Great Date Now
Gary Ferone
Located in Englewood Cliffs and Morristown, NJ
P: 201-735-0005; 973-975-4591
E: gary@greatdatenow.com
W: www.greatdatenow.com

Category: Dating; Coaching; Relationship; Marriage
Company Motto: Personalizes matchmaking for professional, discerning singles

At a glance:
- Service: Clients to Clients; Clients to Members
- Age range: Male clients: 22–75; female clients: 22–70
- Market focus: Professional discerning singles
- Serving: 1) Westchester, Long Island, Manhattan; 2) Bergen, NJ; Fairfield and New Haven, CT
- Number of Clients (paying): 2,000; Members (non-paying): 250
- Pre-screening: Clients: Yes; Members: Yes
- Show pictures: Clients: No; Members: No

Background/Bio:
Tri-state single professionals frequently find themselves frustrated with the process of dating. Great Date Now will help singles find the right relationship by carefully arranging quality dates with singles like them. Privately owned and operated, Great Date Now has developed a new approach to the old-fashioned method of matchmaking. Their clients tell them about the type of person they are looking for and let them do the rest. With personalization and intuition, combined with an outstanding list of single professionals, they will work toward finding the right match for their client.

Process/Personal Style:
Their goal is to remove the discouragement and time consuming efforts so often met with while trying to find that special someone. The bar scene, work environment encounters, and Internet dating can be awkward, disappointing, and depressing. They feel that the personalization in the matchmaking process brings dignity to dating.

Pricing/Service: $$ to $$$

Credentials: MMI Network Member

Master Matchmakers
Joanne and Steven Ward
Established in 1988
Located in Philadelphia, PA 19102
P: 866-To-Match
E: info@mastermatchmakers.com
W: www.mastermatchmakers.com

Category: Dating; Coaching; Relationship; Marriage
Company Motto: A sophisticated way to meet your match

At a glance:
- Service: Clients to Clients
- Age range: Male clients: 25–70; female clients: 25–55
- Market focus: Attractive, successful, relationship-oriented, emotionally and financially secure singles
- Serving: East Coast
- Number of Clients (paying): nearly 1,000 active, current clients
- Pre-screening: Clients: Yes
- Show pictures: Clients: Yes

Background/Bio:
Master Matchmakers has been exclusively introducing vibrant, attractive men and women to each other for over eighteen years. They are high touch, personal "Love Agents™" that specialize in recruiting, and making matches for our exceptionally eligible Client Friends™.

Process/Personal Style:
Their "Love Agents™" will meet a prospective client to get mutually acquainted, discuss possible matches, and retain the service. After a thorough background check they will pursue possible matches for their new Client Friend™ and communicate photos, profiles, and insightful internal commentary between all parties. Upon mutual agreement to meet, they exchange their phone numbers so their Client Friends™ can get acquainted before setting up a date. They require feedback afterwards to gauge their success.

Pricing/Service: $$ to $$$$$
Includes: Coaching, consultation, feedback, personally arranged introductions, select invitations to private special events.

Credentials: MMI Network Member

VIP Life
Lisa Clampitt, CSW, CMM
Established in 2000
Located in New York, NY 10003
P: 212-242-4755
E: lisa@clubviplife.com
W: www.clubviplife.com
Category: Coaching; Relationship; Marriage
Company Motto: An Elite Social Club

At a glance:
- Service: Clients to Members
- Age range: Male clients: 25–65; female members: 21–45
- Market focus: Professional introductions of successful male clients to exceptional, relationship-oriented female members.
- Serving: 1) Connecticut; 2) New York, New Jersey
- Number of Clients (paying): 20; Members (non-paying): 1,000
- Pre-screening: Clients: Yes; Members: Yes
- Show pictures: Clients: Yes; Members: No

Background/Bio:
Lisa Clampitt, CSW, is the founder and president of VIP Life, a professional match-maker and relationship expert since the late 90s and a New York State Certified Social Worker since 1991. Lisa is a natural born matchmaker who constantly introduced her friends to people she felt would be best suited for them, which resulted in many marriages and dozens of children. She has taken her hands-on personal approach and applied her techniques and passion to her professional life of matchmaking.

Process/Personal Style:
A one-on-one personal interview assesses your relationship goals and objective. Male clients review pictures and profiles of female members to assess if this service is right for him. If he decides to join, he receives unlimited introductions to appropriate female members. After each date, feedback is given to assess what worked and what didn't.

Pricing/Service: $$$ to $$$$$
Includes: Unlimited introductions, date and relationship feedback and coaching, concierge services.

Credentials: Certified Matchmaker and Certified Social Worker; MMI Network Member; Member of the Board of Directors of the Professional and Certified Matchmakers Network. **BBB**

135

Catherine's Connections
Kate McCabe
Established in 1998
Located in Greater Manhattan Area
Corporate Office: Stony Creek, CT 06405
P: 212-543-0099; 888-968-5283
E: catherinesconnections@msn.com
W: www.catherinesconnections.com

Category: Dating; Coaching; Relationship; Marriage
Company Motto: Introductions to Mature Mates of Means Over 40™

At a glance:
- Service: Matches Clients to Clients of equal caliber
- Age Range: Male clients: Over 40; female clients: over 40
- Market Focus: Mature Mates of Means and over 40—Jewish and Non-Jewish
- Serving: 1) Tri-State (NY, CT, NJ) 2) Boca and Boston
- Number of Clients (paying): 800; Members (non-paying): 50
- Show pictures Clients: No; Members: No

Background/Bio:
Catherine's background: Went to prep school in New York City. Graduated from Skidmore College. Worked in the fashion field for 10 years. Debut Florida. Currently President of Catherine's Connections last 10 years. Member of Garden Club and The Pine Orchard Yacht and Country Club. Married to Colonel Steven Vass.

Process/Personal Style:
Highly personalized introductions to other members of the same status.

Pricing/Service: $$$$

Credentials: Member of Manhattan Chamber of Commerce; MMI Network Member

Club Elite
Rob Anderson, CMM
Established in 2002
Located in New York, NY 10003
P: 212-242-4755
E: rob@nyclubelite.com
W: www.nyclubelite.com

Category: Dating; Coaching; Relationship
Company Motto: Sophisticated Matchmaking for Exceptional Gay Men

At a glance:
- Service: Clients to Members
- Age range: Male clients: 30–60
- Market focus: Gay men
- Serving: NYC
- Number of Clients (paying): 20; Members (non-paying): 3,000–4,000
- Pre-screening: Clients: Yes; Members: Yes
- Show pictures: Clients: No

Background/Bio:
Rob Anderson is the Director of Club Elite, an exclusive matchmaking service located in New York City for professional gay men looking for long-term relationships. Rob is one of the first matchmakers certified by the Matchmaking Institute and the only gay Certified Matchmaker in the world. As a gay man born and raised in NYC, he has seen first hand struggles that single gay men go through when searching for that special person. This was motivation to become more involved in his community by bringing romance and the possibility of relationships to the lives of professional gay men.

Process/Personal Style:
Rob conducts a lengthy one-on-one interview and creates profiles for all his clients. He hand-selects matches and gets feedback after every date.

Pricing/Service: $ to $$$

Credentials: MMI Network Member

Denise Winston Professional
Matchmaker and Love Coach
Denise Winston
Established in 1987
Located in New York, NY 10021
P: 212-935-9350
E: iwlmatchu@hotmail.com

Category: Dating; Coaching; Relationship; Marriage
Company Motto: In the most confidential, elegant, personal way I will introduce you to the someone special you've been looking for.

At a glance:
- Service: Clients to Members
- Age range: Male clients: 20s to 70; female clients: 20s–70
- Market focus: Professionals, affluent, accomplished
- Serving: 1) NY tri-state area; 2) International
- Number of Clients (paying): 25+; Members (non-paying): 100 (3 times more men than women)
- Pre-screening: Clients: Yes; Members: Yes
- Show pictures: Clients: Yes; Members: Yes

Process/Personal Style:
There is a confidential questionnaire. This includes criminal, financial, medical, marital, DWI, background check. Singles will need to obtain a doctor's note documenting they are in good health, free from infection and communicable diseases, with a copy of the blood workup. Then a personal interview will follow.

Pricing/Service: $$$$$
Includes: Minimum 15 introductions/unlimited advice, counseling, support. Very personalized service. I still do things the old-fashioned way. I am very hands on. I like to know the girls and gentlemen I represent. It is helpful in putting people together when they are friends.

Great Date Now
Gary Ferone
Located in Purchase and Long Island, NY
P: 914-698-8899; 516-673-0777
E: gary@greatdatenow.com
W: www.greatdatenow.com

Category: Dating; Coaching; Relationship; Marriage
Company Motto: Personalizes matchmaking for professional, discerning singles

At a glance:
- Service: Clients to Clients; Clients to Members
- Age range: Male clients: 22–75; female clients: 22–70
- Market focus: Professional discerning singles
- Serving: 1) Westchester, Long Island, Manhattan; 2) Bergen County, NJ; Fairfield and New Haven, CT
- Number of Clients (paying): 2000; Members (non-paying): 250
- Pre-screening: Clients: Yes; Members: Yes
- Show pictures: Clients: No; Members: No

Background/Bio:
Tri-state single professionals frequently find themselves frustrated with the process of dating. Great Date Now will help singles find the right relationship by carefully arranging quality dates with singles like them. Privately owned and operated, Great Date Now has developed a new approach to the old-fashioned method of matchmaking. Their clients tell them about the type of person they are looking for and let them do the rest. With personalization and intuition, combined with an outstanding list of single professionals, they will work toward finding the right match for their client.

Process/Personal Style:
Their goal is to remove the discouragement and time consuming efforts so often met with while trying to find that special someone. The bar scene, work environment encounters, and Internet dating can be awkward, disappointing, and depressing. They feel that the personalization in the matchmaking process brings dignity to dating.

Pricing/Service: $$ to $$$

Credentials: MMI Network Member

Janis Spindel Serious Matchmaking
Janis Spindel
Established in 1993
Located in New York, NY 10028
P: 212-987-1582
E: janis@janisspindelmatchmaker.com
W: www.janisspindelmatchmaker.com

Category: Dating; Coaching; Relationship; Marriage
Company Motto: Where people who wouldn't be caught dead doing this meet others who wouldn't consider it if their lives depended on it.

At a glance:
- Service: Clients to Members
- Age range: ONLY Male clients: 27–70
- Market focus: Upscale, successful, attractive professionals
- Serving: 1) New York, NY; 2) National
- Number of Clients (paying): varies; Members (non-paying): 10,000
- Pre-screening: Clients: Yes; Members: Yes
- Show pictures: Clients: No; Members: No

Background/Bio:
Janis Spindel, a national bestselling author, realized she had a knack for matchmaking back in 1993 when 14 couples she had set up all got married. Since then, she has been providing one-on-one service to upscale professionals and has over 750 marriages to her name.

Process/Personal Style:
A man calls the office first, gets screened, then goes out on a "simulated date" with Janis, discussing what he is looking for, and they decide together if they move forward. Then the process starts!

Pricing/Service: $$$$$

Credentials:

Lunch Appeal
Pamela Stowell, CMM
Established in 2005
Located in Liverpool, NY 13088
P: 315-453-5600
E: pam@lunchappeal.com
W: www.lunchappeal.com

Category: Dating
Company Motto: We put the "FUN" back in dating!

At a glance:
- Service: Clients to Clients
- Age Range: Male clients: 25–70; female clients: 21–68
- Market focus: Busy, active professionals
- Serving: Upstate New York area
- Number of Clients (paying): 250+
- Pre-screening: Clients: Yes
- Show pictures: Clients: No

Background/Bio:
Pam has been blessed with a strong marriage and great family life. She's been married for 15 years and has a 14 year old son.

How and why you became a matchmaker:
Because it is very difficult for singles to meet people due to their busy schedules, Pam looked for alternatives to online dating. When she saw there weren't any options, she decided to focus on helping the singles market.

Process/Personal Style:
Lunch Appeal provides a very professional, discreet atmosphere where the customer can share what is important to them in a relationship and in a mate. They hand-select matches after meeting everyone one-on-one and get feedback from each introduction.

Pricing/Service: $
Includes: Guaranteed dates, background checks, feedback from each date, access to hundreds of singles, invites to private singles events, set up entire first date, and the comfort of knowing their matches were based upon many layers of compatibility.

Credentials: MMI Network Member **BBB**

Master Matchmakers
Joanne and Steven Ward
Established in 1988
Located in Philadelphia, PA 19102
P: 866-To-Match
E: info@mastermatchmakers.com
W: www.mastermatchmakers.com

Category: Dating; Coaching; Relationship; Marriage
Company Motto: A sophisticated way to meet your match

At a glance:
- Service: Clients to Clients
- Age range: Male clients: 25–70; female clients: 25–55
- Market focus: Attractive, successful, relationship oriented, emotionally and financially secure singles
- Serving: East Coast
- Number of Clients (paying): nearly 1,000 active, current clients
- Pre-screening: Clients: Yes
- Show pictures: Clients: Yes

Background/Bio:
Master Matchmakers has been exclusively introducing vibrant, attractive men and women to each other for over eighteen years. They are high touch, personal "Love Agents™" that specialize in recruiting, and making matches for our exceptionally eligible Client Friends™.

Process/Personal Style:
Their "Love Agents™ will meet a prospective client to get mutually acquainted, discuss possible matches, and retain the service. After a thorough background check they will pursue possible matches for their new Client Friend™ and communicate photos, profiles, and insightful internal commentary between all parties. Upon mutual agreement to meet, they exchange their phone numbers so their Client Friends™ can get acquainted before setting up a date. They require feedback afterwards to gauge their success.

Pricing/Service: $$ to $$$$$
Includes: Coaching, consultation, feedback, personally arranged introductions, select invitations to private special events.

Credentials: MMI Network Member

VIP Life
Lisa Clampitt, CSW, CMM
Established in 2000
Located in New York, NY 10003
P: 212-242-4755
E: lisa@clubviplife.com
W: www.clubviplife.com

Category: Coaching; Relationship; Marriage
Company Motto: An Elite Social Club

At a glance:
- Service: Clients to Members
- Age range: Male clients: 25–65; female members: 21–45
- Market focus: Professional introductions of successful male clients to exceptional, relationship-oriented female members.
- Serving: 1) Connecticut; 2) New York, New Jersey
- Number of Clients (paying): 20; Members (non-paying): 1,000
- Pre-screening: Clients: Yes; Members: Yes
- Show pictures: Clients: Yes; Members: No

Background/Bio:
Lisa Clampitt, CSW, is the founder and president of VIP Life, a professional match-maker and relationship expert since the late 90s and a New York State Certified Social Worker since 1991. Lisa is a natural born matchmaker who constantly introduced her friends to people she felt would be best suited for them, which resulted in many marriages and dozens of children. She has taken her hands-on personal approach and applied her techniques and passion to her professional life of matchmaking.

Process/Personal Style:
A one-on-one personal interview assesses your relationship goals and objective. Male clients review pictures and profiles of female members to assess if this service is right for him. If he decides to join, he receives unlimited introductions to appropriate female members. After each date, feedback is given to assess what worked and what didn't.

Pricing/Service: $$$ to $$$$$
Includes: Unlimited introductions, date and relationship feedback and coaching, concierge services.

Credentials: Certified Matchmaker and Certified Social Worker; MMI Network Member; Member of the Board of Directors of the Professional and Certified Matchmakers Network.

Dating Directions
Susie Hardesty, CMM
Elizabeth Cobey-Piper, CMM
Established in 2003
Located in Columbus, Ohio
P: 614-784-8188
E: info@datingdirections.com
W: www.datingdirections.com

Category: Dating; Coaching
Company Motto: Personalized service for exceptional results

At a glance:
- Service: Clients to Members
- Age range: Male clients: 30–75; female clients: 25–65
- Market focus: Professionals
- Serving: 1) Ohio; 2) national clientele
- Number of Clients (paying) 30; Members (non-paying): 500
- Pre-Screening: Clients: Yes; Members: Yes
- Show pictures: Clients: Yes; Members: No

Background/Bio:
Certified Matchmaker Elizabeth Cobey-Piper is an experienced and dedicated dating coach and successful matchmaker. She works closely with her clients developing strategies for realizing their dating and relationship goals. Elizabeth's successful 20-year career in marketing, training, and coaching has prepared her for working with singles in a positive and proactive way. Her clients enjoy her powerful and personal approach to helping them meet just the right person and developing the relationship of a lifetime.

Certified Matchmaker Susie Hardesty is an exceptional matchmaker with 14 years of experience and hundreds of happy clients matched. Her intuitive approach coupled with her personalized service gives her a success rate well above industry standards.

Process/Personal Style:
They specialize in quality clients who are looking for exceptional relationships. They work very personally with every client to help him/her reach his/her dating goals. As a result, their clients are finding love and committed relationships.

Pricing/Service: $$$$

Credentials: MMI Network Member

Lunch Date
Mike Green
Established in 1995
Located in Cleveland, OH 44115
P: 216-687-8139
E: date@lunchdate.com
W: www.lunchdate.com

Category: Dating; Coaching; Relationship; Marriage
Company Motto: Personalized matchmaking at its finest.

At a glance:
- Service: Clients to Clients
- Age Range: Male clients: 23–75; female clients: 22–75
- Market focus: Single educated professionals
- Serving: Cleveland, Akron (northeast Ohio)
- Number of Clients (paying): 750
- Pre-screening: Clients: Yes
- Show pictures: Clients: No

Background/Bio:
Lunch Date is a privately owned dating service for single professionals. Established in 1995, Lunch Date provides a personalized service unmatched in its industry. The owner personally meets every client and is responsible for the matchmaking. All dates are coordinated by our staff and take place in a casual manner, which can be coffee, lunch, or a drink.

How and why you became a matchmaker:
Having strong interpersonal skills along with the ability to assess people, I thought it would be a great idea to start a personalized dating service. People rely on my insight and guidance as they begin their search for a relationship. I enjoy helping people to find relationships that ultimately bring them happiness.

Process/Personal Style:
I meet clients personally to compile their profile. I then make selections from the database that matches clients' criteria. We contact clients to present our selection and if there is interest we then contact the other client to arrange the date. Feedback is very important as it helps us fine-tune our choices for future dates. Our strength is that we know our clients well, which equates to effective matchmaking.

Pricing/Service: $

Credentials:

Singles Station Dating Company
Charlee Brotherton, CMM
Established in 1979
Located in Tulsa, OK 74136
P: 918-491-0002
E: info@singlesstation.com
W: www.singlesstation.com

Category: Dating; Coaching; Relationship; Marriage
Company Motto: True Love Starts Right Here!

At a glance:
- Service: Clients to Clients
- Age range: Male clients: 25–85; female clients: 21–80
- Market focus: Professionals, Christian and Secular
- Serving: 1) Tulsa and Oklahoma City, OK; 2) Little Rock, Bentonville, and Fort Smith, AK; Nashville, TN
- Number of Clients (paying): 10,000; Members (non-paying): 100
- Pre-screening: Clients: Yes; Members: Yes
- Show pictures: to Clients: No; Members: No

Background/Bio:
The Singles Station Dating Company has a 25-year reputation of helping discerning singles find romantic companionship. It has introduced more than 100,000 couples and is responsible for thousands of successful relationships and marriages.

Process/Personal Style:
They meet with potential clients for a personal interview in their offices. Clients complete a comprehensive profile and a personality profile. In addition, they are screened for felony convictions, history of mental illness and drug or alcohol abuse. After every introduction, each client calls with feedback on their date to member services and decides if they would like another introduction or to continue to date the person they just met.

Pricing/Service: $$ and up

Credentials: Member of the Board of Directors of the Professional and Certified Matchmakers Network; MMI Network Member

Date Nite
Tobi Quinlan, CMM
Established in 2003
Located in Kennett Square, PA 19348
P: 610-220-5206
E: info@dateniteinc.com
W: www.dateniteinc.com

Category: Dating; Coaching
Company Motto: Meet your future

At a glance:
- Service: Clients to Clients; Clients to Members
- Age range: Male clients: 25–65; female clients: 25–65
- Market focus: Professional singles
- Serving: Pennsylvania
- Number of Clients (paying): 150; Members (non-paying): 150
- Pre-screening: Clients: Yes; Members: Yes
- Show pictures: Clients: Yes; Members: Yes

Background/Bio:
Tobi graduated from Bucknell University in 1990 and received a BA in Economics. She worked for 10 years in NYC for Accenture. She was a senior manager and led large-scale technology projects at investment banking clients. After she left NYC, she worked for Deutsche Bank and Strategic Systems Solutions as a technology consultant. She also rides horses and has competed at large hunter/jumper horse shows from Florida to Vermont.

Process/Personal Style:
Date Nite provides a safe, personalized, low pressure introduction service to professional singles. We build a trusting relationship with our clients and relieve them of the time consuming part of finding a match and let them focus on the fun part ... the dating! Clients talk on the phone before meeting someone on a date, and we perform follow-ups after the date and give each side feedback. Let us help you meet your future.

Pricing/Service: $

Credentials: MMI Network Member

Master Matchmakers
Joanne and Steven Ward
Established since 1988
Located in Philadelphia, PA 19102
P: 866-To-Match
E: info@mastermatchmakers.com
W: www.mastermatchmakers.com

Category: Dating; Coaching; Relationship; Marriage
Company Motto: A sophisticated way to meet your match

At a glance:
- Service: Clients to Clients
- Age range: Male clients: 25–70; female clients: 25–55
- Market focus: Attractive, successful, relationship oriented, emotionally and financially secure singles
- Serving: East Coast
- Number of Clients (paying): nearly 1,000 active, current clients
- Pre-screening: Clients: Yes
- Show pictures: Clients: Yes

Background/Bio:
Master Matchmakers has been exclusively introducing vibrant, attractive men and women to each other for over eighteen years. They are high touch, personal "Love Agents™" that specialize in recruiting, and making matches for our exceptionally eligible Client Friends™.

Process/Personal Style:
Their "Love Agents™" will meet a prospective client to get mutually acquainted, discuss possible matches, and retain the service. After a thorough background check they will pursue possible matches for their new Client Friend™ and communicate photos, profiles, and insightful internal commentary between all parties. Upon mutual agreement to meet, they exchange their phone numbers so their Client Friends™ can get acquainted before setting up a date. They require feedback afterwards to gauge their success.

Pricing/Service: $$ to $$$$$
Includes: Coaching, consultation, feedback, personally arranged introductions, select invitations to private special events.

Credentials: MMI Network Member

Options
Steve & Naomi
Established in 1994
Located in Philadelphia, PA 19103
P: 800-360-3283
E: rp@optionsdate.com
W: www.optionsdate.com & www.gayoptions.com

Category: Dating; Relationship; Marriage
Company Motto: Personalized matchmaking for those seeking quality relationships.

At a glance:
- Service: Clients to Clients
- Age range: Male clients: 21–80s; female clients: 21–80s
- Market focus: professionals; self-employed; heterosexuals; gays and lesbians
- Serving: 1) South Florida; 2) Los Angeles, CA; VA, DC, MD, DE, PA, NJ, NYC, Long Island, Lower CT, GA, and AL
- Number of Clients (paying): 11,000+
- Pre-screening: Clients: Yes
- Show pictures: Clients: No

Background/Bio:
The two owners have over 35 years of combined experience in the dating industry. Steve has a Masters in aerospace engineering and handles the back end of the business while Naomi has been passionately matching since 1983. The couple met in 1997, got married, and have been jointly running Options dating service ever since.

Process/Personal Style:
A personalized offline dating service with matches based on compatibility and physical qualities. All applicants are screened in person with all vital information and personal statistics guaranteed. All new applicants must undergo a background check.

Pricing/Service: $$ to $$$

Credentials: **BBB**

The Relationship Company
Established in 2000
Located in Columbia, SC 29201
P: 803-251-8754
E: membershipservices@btitelecom.net
W: www.therelationshipcompany.net

Category: Dating
Company Motto: Live the life you imagined!

At a glance:
- Service: Clients to Clients
- Serving: South Carolina
- Number of Clients (paying): 3,000
- Pre-screening: Clients: Yes
- Show pictures: Clients: No
- Privacy: High

Background/Bio:
Our relationship consultants have an extensive resume in the field of introduction services. Our consultants have a minimum of 12 years experience and varied degrees of education.

Process/Personal Style:
Each member will meet with a relationship consultant to determine if they are eligible to enroll and if we are able to accommodate their expectations. Each new member completes a series of tests to determine personality traits that are vital in the matching process to ensure a high degree of compatibility. Each member will then be matched accordingly and work one on one with their consultant to further understand their needs and continue to make introductions.

Pricing/Service: $

Credentials: **BBB**

Matchmaker International
Shane Hollifield
Established in 1988
Located in Knoxville, TN
P: 865-588-1770
E: info@matchmakerintl.net
W: www.matchmakerintl.net

Category: Dating; Coaching; Relationship; Marriage

At a glance:
- Service: Clients to Clients
- Market focus: No prejudice against anyone
- Serving: Knoxville, TN; Johnson City, TN
- Number of Clients (paying): 5,000
- Pre-Screening: Clients: Yes
- Show pictures: Clients: No

Background/Bio:
Owner has been in industry for 17 years making over 767 marriages. He is still the only owner that still meets the people/clients.

Process/Personal Style:
They run a full police background check of every client along with confirming marital status. So they meet and screen each client thoroughly.

Pricing/Service: $ to $$
Includes: Each membership is custom-tailored to each person so its features can vary based upon what they are looking for.

Credentials: **BBB**

Singles Station Dating Company
Charlee Brotherton, CMM
Established in 1979
Located in Bentonville, Fort Smith and Little Rock
P: 501-255-LOVE
E: info@singlesstation.com
W: www.singlesstation.com

Category: Dating; Coaching; Relationship; Marriage
Company Motto: True Love Starts Right Here!

At a glance:
- Service: Clients to Clients
- Age range: Male clients: 25–85; female clients: 21–80
- Market focus: Professionals, Christian and Secular
- Serving: 1) Little Rock, Bentonville and Fort Smith, Arkansas; 2) Tulsa and Oklahoma City, OK, Nashville, Tennessee
- Number of Clients (paying): 10,000; Members (non-paying): 100
- Pre-Screening: Clients: Yes; Members: Yes
- Show pictures: to Clients: No; Members: No

Background/Bio:
The Singles Station Dating Company has a 25-year reputation of helping discerning singles find romantic companionship. It has introduced more than 100,000 couples and is responsible for thousands of successful relationships and marriages.

Process/Personal Style:
They meet with potential clients for a personal interview in their offices. Clients complete a comprehensive profile and a personality profile. In addition, they are screened for felony convictions, history of mental illness and drug or alcohol abuse. After every introduction, each client calls with feedback of their date to member services and decides if they would like another introduction or continue to date the person they just met.

Pricing/Service: $$ and up

Credentials: Member of the Board of Directors of the Professional and Certified Matchmakers; Network MMI Network Member

Kelleher & Associates, Inc.
Amber Kelleher
Established in 1986
Located in Dallas, TX
P: 800-401-MATCH (6282)
E: info@kelleher-associates.com
W: www.meettheelite.com

Category: Dating; Coaching; Relationship; Marriage
Company Motto: Exquisite matchmaking since 1986.

At a glance:
- Service: Clients to Clients; Clients to Members
- Age range: Male clients: 25 and up; female clients: 25 and up
- Market focus: Busy professionals and affluent entrepreneurs nationwide
- Serving: 1) Scottsdale; 2) California, Chicago, West Palm Beach, Dallas, Las Vegas, and New York
- Pre-screening: Clients: Yes; Members: Yes
- Show pictures: Clients: Yes; Members: No

Background/Bio:
The ultra-exclusive mother–daughter matchmaking team of Kelleher & Associates was founded by Jill Kelleher in 1986. Kelleher & Associates caters to an exceptional clientele. Noted as a National Search Firm, we represent the best and brightest in the U.S. as well as abroad. We are distinguished by our stellar reputation, priority on discretion, and a proprietary database, resulting from over two decades in our industry. Boasting a staff of over 30 full-time matchmakers nationwide with domestic offices that include New York, San Francisco, Beverly Hills, Scottsdale, La Jolla, West Palm Beach, Dallas, Las Vegas, Chicago, and Silicon Valley.

Process/Personal Style:
Once an applicant is successfully accepted, Kelleher clients are provided with a very unique, personalized service like no other. Each of their introductions are hand-selected with great detail and are based on their client's specific criteria. Kelleher & Associates set the standard for matchmaking over 20 years ago, and continues to do so today.

Pricing/Service: $$$$ to $$$$$
Includes: One full year of quality introductions, with additional year of hold extensions. Custom memberships may also include relationship experts, psychiatrists, and life coaches.

Credentials: **BBB**

153

Selective Search, Inc.
Barbie Adler
Established in 2000
Located in Dallas, TX
P: 866-592-1200
E: barbie@selectivesearch-inc.com
W: www.selectivesearch-inc.com

Category: Coaching; Relationship; Marriage
Company Motto: Elite matchmakers to the most eligible, commitment-minded bachelors.

At a glance:
- Service: Clients to Members
- Market focus: affluent professionals
- Serving: 1) Phoenix, AZ; 2) Chicago, New York, Los Angeles, Orange County, San Francisco, Atlanta, Dallas, Miami, Washington, DC, St. Louis
- Number of Clients (paying): 100; Members (non-paying): 50,000
- Pre-screening: Clients: Yes; Members: Yes
- Show pictures: Clients: Yes; Members: upon request

Background/Bio:
Barbie Adler, founder and president of Selective Search, one the leading off-line personal matchmaking firms with clients across the country, is one of the industry's most respected matchmakers, sought-after lifestyle management coach and personal relationship expert. Profiled as an authority on relationships by *Forbes, Fortune, The Economist, The Wall Street Journal, USA Today, Self, Men's Heath,* and CNN, among others, Barbie's expertise in the matchmaking world is in high demand.

Process/Personal Style:
Exclusive within the industry, Selective Search represents a new paradigm in matchmaking, that of the "executive recruiter." The approach, the process, and the results are unique to Selective Search and are a testament to Barbie's vision of helping individuals find each other in a very personal, yet effective and efficient environment.

Pricing/Service: $$$$$
Includes: One year membership, ten introductions

Credentials: MMI Network Member

Compatibles
Nicole T. Leclerc
Established since 1987
Located in Colchester, VT 05446
P: 802-872-8500
E: Nicole@compatibles.com
W: www.compatibles.com

Category: Dating; Coaching
Company Motto: Your direction to connection

At a glance:
- Service: Clients to Clients
- Age range: Male clients: 25–70; female clients: 25–60
- Market focus: Non-smoking professionals in Vermont
- Serving: Vermont
- Number of Clients (paying): 275; Members (non-paying): 5
- Pre-screening: Clients: Yes; Members: No
- Show pictures: Clients: Yes; Members: No

Background/Bio
Compatibles is a personalized, traditional matchmaking service for busy professionals throughout Vermont. It is a 19 year old company with a proven track record of attracting quality clients. Its reputation for one-on-one matchmaker/client process, exceptional clientele and affordability are its strengths.

Process/Personal Style:
Nicole meets with all her clients face-to-face for an initial interview. Gathering information about the client and their preferences and criteria, she is armed with the information she needs to generate a few initial introductions. After each introduction, the clients provide feedback to her on a multitude of aspects which enables Nicole to get closer and closer to hitting the mark where chemistry blooms between two people.

Pricing/Service: $
Includes: A book, one to three referrals per month during membership term. Dating advice, coaching, hand-holding and quarterly e-mails alerting them to dating/singles events within Vermont.

Credentials:

Options
Steve & Naomi
Established since 1994
Located in Vienna, VA
P: 800-360-3283
E: rp@optionsdate.com
W: www.optionsdate.com & www.gayoptions.com

Category: Dating; Relationship; Marriage
Company Motto: Personalized matchmaking for those seeking quality relationships.

At a glance:
* Service: Clients to Clients
* Age range: Male clients: 21–80s; female clients: 21–80s
* Market focus: professionals; self-employed; heterosexuals; gays and lesbians
* Serving: 1) South Florida; 2) Los Angeles, CA; VA, DC, MD, DE, PA, NJ, NYC, Long Island, Lower CT, GA, and AL
* Number of Clients (paying): 11,000+
* Pre-screening: Clients: Yes
* Show pictures: Clients: No

Background/Bio:
The two owners have over 35 years of combined experience in the dating industry. Steve has a Masters in aerospace engineering and handles the back end of the business while Naomi has been passionately matching since 1983. The couple met in 1997, got married, and have been jointly running Options dating service ever since.

Process/Personal Style:
A personalized offline dating service with matches based on compatibility and physical qualities. All applicants are screened in person with all vital information and personal statistics guaranteed. All new applicants must undergo a background check.

Pricing/Service: $$ to $$$

Credentials: **BBB**

It Takes 2
Carrie Daichman
Established in 1998
Located in Glenallen, VA
P: 804-967-9911
E: meetright1@aol.com
W: www.ittakes2online.com

Category: Dating; Coaching; Relationship; Marriage
Company Motto: It takes 2 to help you meet just the right 1

At a glance:
- Service: Clients to Clients
- Age range: Male clients: 21+; female clients: 21+
- Market focus: Professionals
- Serving: Central Virginia
- Number of Clients (paying): 3,000+
- Pre-Screening: Clients: Yes
- Show pictures: Clients:

Background/Bio:
14 years experience averaging two to three client marriages per month.

Process/Personal Style:
We offer a free consultation. We do not use video or computers. It takes two matches individuals based on compatibility using personality assessments. We do screen all of our clients.

Pricing/Service: $

Credentials: **BBB**

157

Elite Love Registry, LLC
Kailen Rosenberg
Established since 2006
Located in Seattle, WA
P: 877-930-5683
E: kailenluv@aol.com
W: www.eliteloveregistry.com

Category: Dating; Coaching; Relationship; Marriage
Company Motto: Where healthy relationships begin.

At a glance:
- Service: Clients to Clients; Clients to Members; Clients to Subscribers
- Age range: Male and female clients: late 20s to mid 70s
- Market focus: all, yet elite and healthy-minded "most eligible in the country"
- Serving: 1) Atlanta; 2) Chicago, Minnesota, Dallas, Las Vegas, New York, Seattle, Cincinnati, Denver, Los Angeles, Scottsdale, Washington, DC, and international locatons
- Number of Clients (paying): hundreds; Members (non-paying): thousands
- Pre-screening: Clients: Yes; Members: Yes
- Show pictures: Clients: Yes; Members: No

Background/Bio:
Kailen Rosenberg is a nationally recognized and sought after relationship expert and life designer to the elite. Over 15 years ago, Kailen designed a methodology based on certain principles, proven to create true elegance and success in the personal lives of healthy-minded, busy, successful individuals around the globe. She is a respected innovator in her field and is celebrity endorsed and supported by nationally acclaimed experts. Kailen has been recognized for "doing it ethically" by the *Seattle Times*.

Process/Personal Style:
Their members are highly pre-screened and background checked. To provide a safe and secure experience for their members, all potential members must pass a three-step screening process, and are only selected after a personal face-to-face interview has occurred.

Pricing/Service: $ to $$$$
Includes: A phone interview, a face-to-face assessment, an extensive background and identity check, love and self-image blue prints with a personal love architect™.

Dinner Works
Susan Kates, CMM
Established in 2005
Located in Sheldrake Blvd. Toronto
P: 416-483-1312
E: toronto@dinnerworks.ca
W: www.dinnerworks.ca

Category: Dating
Company Motto: A personalized service like no other.

At a glance:
• Service: Clients to Members
• Age range: Male clients: 25–60; female clients: 25–55
• Market focus: Professionals
• Serving: Toronto and surrounding area
• Number of Clients: 12,000+
• Pre-screening: Clients: Yes; Members: Yes
• Show pictures: Clients: Yes; Members: Yes
• Privacy: High

Background/Bio:
Susan Kates is totally passionate about her business. She is a woman with high integrity and only wants to take on clients where she can deliver results. She will work hard for her clients and her clients are appreciative of the work she does. She is an excellent listener and uses her years of marketing experience to make connections.

Process/Personal Style:
Susan conducts a personal interview with her clients where she gets to know them as people. Susan looks into the soul of her clients and that's what she tries to portray when she is trying to find a match.

Pricing/Service: $$

Credentials: MMI Network Member

Like Fine Wine
Evelyn Lazare, M.B.A.
Established since 2006
Located in Vancouver, British Columbia, Canada
P: 604-669-4560
E: info@likefinewineintroductions.ca
W: www.likefinewineintroductions.ca

Category: Coaching, Relationship; Marriage
Company Motto: Introductions with integrity exclusively for people in their 40s, 50s, and 60s.

At a glance:
- Service: Clients to Clients
- Age range: Male clients: 40–69; female clients: 40–69
- Market focus: Successful, accomplished professionals, academics and entrepreneurs, whether still working, retired or semi-retired.
- Serving: Greater Vancouver area
- Number of Clients (paying): all
- Pre-screening: Clients: Yes
- Show pictures: Clients: Yes

Background/Bio:
Like Fine Wine offers personal and professional introductions to people in their 40s, 50s and 60s, in and around Greater Vancouver. They are the only introduction service catering exclusively to this demographic. Their screening ensures that clients are all serious about finding a long-term relationship.

Process/Personal Style:
The first step is a consultation in the client's home. They ask over 150 questions, most of them open-ended. They then prepare a narrative profile, accompanied by photos taken by their professional photographer. They have a frank discussion with each person before making an introduction and follow up after each first date.

Pricing/Service: $$
Includes: Face-to-face consultation, session with professional photographer, telephone discussions prior to and following up on introductions, dating coaching, (if requested).

Credentials: MMI Network Member

Misty River Introductions
Linda Miller
Established in 1995, matching since 1993
Located in Ontario, Canada (Ottawa Area)
P: 613-257-3531; 416-777-6302; 705-734-1292;
519-658-4204; 514-879-0573
E: matchcan@ca.inter.net
W: www.mistyriverintros.com

Category: Dating; Coaching; Relationship; Marriage
Company Motto: Traditional matchmaking for singles looking for long-term relationships

At a glance:
- Service: Clients to Clients
- Age range: Male clients: 25+; female clients: 23+
- Market focus: We have clients from all walks of life, all religions, and all socio-economic groups
- Serving: 1) All of Ontario; 2) Quebec and Northern New York State
- Number of Clients (paying): 10,000
- Pre-screening: Clients: Yes
- Show pictures: Clients: Yes
- Privacy: High

Background/Bio:
Linda Miller is the owner of the service and meets with each client for a free consultation to determine the prospective client's suitability for the service. Linda Miller has been matching successfully for 14 years. She has a background in psychology and management.

Process/Personal Style:
Clients can expect to have matches presented on a weekly basis unless otherwise informed (such as in cases where very detailed, specific criteria are evident). Linda is hands-on in the meeting and matching process. She still oversees almost all the matching, but the contact information is done through each client's individual liaison.

Pricing/Service: $$
Includes: Some packages include photos as part of the cost, some do not include photos and are charged as extras, all packages come with a different hold period depending on what the client chooses

Real Connections
Elizabeth MacInnis, CMM
Established in 2006
Located in Edmonton, Alberta, Canada
P: 780-819-7325
E: elizabeth@connectingrealpeople.com
W: www.connectingrealpeople.com

Category: Dating; Coaching; Relationship
Company Motto: If you're true to yourself, you will find a long-term, committed relationship

At a glance:
- Service: Clients to Subscribers
- Age range: Male clients: 28–55; female clients: 46–52
- Market focus: Professionals
- Serving: Northern Alberta region (primary Edmonton, secondary surrounding areas)
- Number of Clients (paying): 7
- Pre-screening: Clients: Yes
- Show pictures: Clients: No

Background/Bio:
Elizabeth has a human resources background. She originally set out to study social work but soon found out that it was difficult to deal with individuals who were not happy all the time. She decided to have a family and settle down. She found herself divorced and didn't like the single and looking life. She re-educated herself in marketing/human resources. She became a successful sales consultant and now works in both the human resources and sales fields.

Process/Personal Style:
Elizabeth believes members should always feel like she works only for them. Elizabeth is attentive to their needs and so she is available to speak with them. Her clients always know that honesty is the biggest factor, and it is an expectation she has of them as well as of herself.

Pricing/Service: $$
Includes: Personal, one-on-one service, scheduled dates, full interview with analysis and profile, security and credit check, feedback on dates, VIP status on dates, VIP status for E-newsletters, VIP status for gift giveaways and promotions, VIP status for all Real Connections events

Credentials: MMI Network Member

Rate Your Matchmaker!

Visit www.matchmakinginstitute.com/survey, enter your matchmaker ID (as listed at the bottom of each matchmaker profile), and add your review and rating.

If you do not see a matchmaker or introduction service you've been working with listed, feel free to add them.

Please note that not all of the matchmakers listed in this guide are approved by the Matchmaking Institute or are a part of the Matchmaking Institute's Professional and Certified Network. This listing is provided to you purely as a resource so you can learn about and understand the different types of matchmakers available to you. This listing will provide you with samples of different styles and business models. Because we do not know each and every matchmaker, each submission, review and rating will be carefully reviewed by the Matchmaking Institute and will help us monitor matchmakers and maintain a strict code of ethics in the matchmaker industry.

Adding your reviews will therefore help us improve our guide for future editions.

Thank you.

Part III

Additional Materials

Matchmakers Multiple Listing Service (MMLS)

The Matchmaking Institute is committed to introducing singles to Certified and Professional Matchmakers in a confidential, safe, and secure manner, while providing information that may assist their decision-making process.

Let a Certified and Professional Matchmaker find you a Match!

We created the Matchmakers Multiple Listing Service for this very reason; this confidential Singles Database is used by Certified and Professional Matchmakers worldwide to search for potential matches for their clients. If you decide to list your profile, you could be matched with one of their clients.

Many singles contact us daily, either looking to hire a matchmaker or requesting to be posted on our Matchmaker Multiple Listing Service (MMLS), where they are pre-screened and background checked.

The MMLS concept is similar to the Real Estate MLS. The real estate industry has used this idea since the early 1970s, and could not survive without it. The MMLS gives you great exposure to a pool of matchmakers always searching for matches for their clients.

If you do not yet feel ready to hire a personal matchmaker, this is a great way to start.

How does it work? Certified and Professional Matchmakers have a private access to the Multiple Listing Service. This access is totally confidential and secured. Information is made available to matchmakers only and can be removed at your request at any time. None of your information will be released to marketers or made public.

Find the Certified Matchmaker that is right for you!

If you are ready to hire a Certified and Professional Matchmaker, we can help you find a proper matchmaker near you who will assist you on a one-on-one basis.

Tell us a bit about yourself and we will arrange for a phone or e-mail introduction to an appropriate Certified Matchmaker. You do not pay a fee for this introduction.

Feel free to contact us at makemeamatch@matchmakinginstitute.com or visit us online at:

www.matchmakinginstitute.com/singles

Matchmaking Institute's Professional and Certified Matchmakers Network

The Matchmaking Institute has established the very first worldwide Matchmakers Network of Professional and Certified Matchmakers.

This network allows matchmakers across the country to pool their resources to facilitate matches internationally.

On a larger scale, a major goal of the network is to mainstream the matchmaking industry by removing the stigma and mystery historically attached to it.

www.matchmakinginstitute.com/network/

Professional and Certified Matchmakers Network Board of Directors

Lisa Clampitt - New York, NY - Chairman of the Board

Lisa Clampitt, CSW, is the cofounder and executive director of the Matchmaking Institute, a professional matchmaker and a New York State Certified Social Worker for over 15 years. She was educated at New York University, receiving a BA in Dramatic Literature, and received her graduate degree, a Masters in Social Work, from the University of Michigan.

Lisa has had many years of experience in individual and couples counseling as well as relationship and date coaching and has owned her own very successful matchmaking company, VIP Life, for over six years. With this experience and an extensive knowledge of the matchmaking industry under her belt, she went on to create the Matchmaking Institute in order to train and certify others, establishing a strict code of ethics in this important industry. Lisa is consistently sought after as a matchmaking and relationship expert and has had extensive international press coverage, including The O'Reilly Factor, ABC's *20/20*, The *New York Times*, Fox News Live, WNBC's *Today in New York*, *Time* magazine, Forbes.com, *O! The Magazine*, *Men's Health Journal* and *Cosmopolitan*.

Charlee Brotherton - Tulsa, OK

Charlee Brotherton is a CPA, a Matchmaker of Brotherton & Associates Introductions, Inc., and owner and CEO of the Singles Station. She has been in the matchmaking business for over seven years. She acquired the Singles Station Dating Company in January 2000 and has expanded the service to include six offices in Tulsa, Oklahoma City, Bentonville, Fort Smith, Little Rock, and Nashville.

She personally matches clients as well as manages the introductions for thousands of singles through the Singles Station Dating Company When she was first introduced to the matchmaking/dating service concept, she loved the idea. Being a Certified Public Accountant, she has a quantitative, logical thought process. It made perfect sense for her to take an organized approach to meeting the person you would spend the rest of your life with. Most singles employ a haphazard approach to meeting singles. Singles spend more time thinking about the features they want on a new car than the attributes that they are looking for in a life-long mate. Picking the right mate is the most important decision you will ever make.

Julie Ferman - Los Angeles, CA

Matchmaker, dating industry consultant, media personality, speaker, and writer, Julie Ferman founded Cupid's Coach in December 2000. Julie's passion in life is bringing people together. Above all, she values human connection, lives touching lives. As Cupid's Coach, she specializes in helping singles make that all-important initial connection with the right people.

TV and Radio have long been comfort zones for Julie; her television appearances include NBC's *Life Moments,* The Discovery Channel's *Berman and Berman Show,* and a dozen network news programs in Los Angeles. Among the scores of newspaper articles are the *Los Angeles Times,* the *Wall Street Journal,* the *Dallas Morning News,* and the *St. Louis Post Dispatch.* Julie is responsible for over 1,000 marriages. She knows the love business. She has degrees in psychology and human sexuality, and has spent eight years in sales and marketing with the hospitality industry. Currently she spends her time serving and bringing together relationship-oriented people.

Violet Lim - Singapore

Violet Lim studied law at the University of Manchester and also holds a Masters degree in Industrial Relations from the London School of Economics. Violet's former career in international finance left her personally unsatisfied, so she and her husband, Jamie Lee, decided to forfeit their stable incomes to start their own business in the dating world. Violet and her husband met while he was working towards a degree in accounting and finance. The couple's first date was over lunch—lunch being the underlying theme for Lunch Actually.

In 2004, Violet became the first Asian to become certified by the Matchmaking Institute. In April of that same year, Lunch Actually Singapore opened. The second office, in Kuala Lumpur, Malaysia, came along a year and a half later. The Singapore office serves over one thousand members while the Kuala Lumpur office currently has over 150 members.

Certification

The Matchmaking Institute offers a certification program which is a highly specified curriculum of classes put together to
teach matchmakers matchmaking skills as well as provide all the tools needed to become a Certified Matchmaker and run a business in the matchmaking industry with credentials.

The Matchmaking Institute, following a strict code of ethics and standards, established a program in 2003 designed to train those who wish to become Certified Matchmakers, while providing practical knowledge that will improve the way to start a matchmaking business.

When matchmakers get trained and certified, they gain knowledge and support.

Sample Certificate

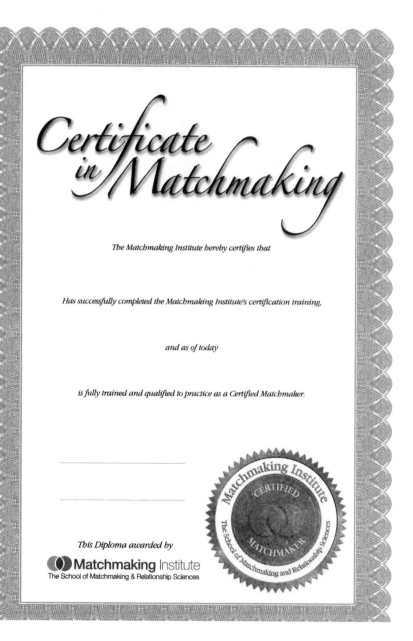

What is a Certified Matchmaker?

**A Certified Matchmaker is a
trained and accredited individual who:**
- adheres to the highest quality standards in the industry
- follows a strict code of ethics
- is dedicated to a client's right to a personal, supportive, and professional service at all times
- maintains strict confidentiality of all clients' accounts and will not divulge, discuss, or otherwise exploit any restricted material related to client profile, status, or record of activity
- takes utmost care to deliver the highest standard of service for total customer satisfaction and will be subject to quarterly evaluations correlative to client assessments
- responds to clients' inquires in a timely fashion and offers complete and clear answers
- is diligent when qualifying all potential matches on behalf of their clients with a personalized approach from beginning to end
- is subject to additional mandatory training and professional development for annual re-certification, in accordance with the Matchmaking Institute's guidelines

A Certified Matchmaker:
- is recommended by an industry authority
- is a trained professional and meets ethical standards
- provides clients with the highest standard of care
- is held accountable for the quality of her/his service
- is reviewed and audited based on client feedback submissions
- is part of a network that provides the most updated information to keep up with the highest level of service
- is subject to mandatory re-certification

Versus

An uncertified matchmaker:
- has no industry recommendations
- may have no references apart from clients and friends
- has no affiliation with any reporting agency that can take action
- has no credentials from an independent authority
- is not required to follow a code of ethics
- has no accountability to anyone to provide a good service
- provides no guarantee of customer service
- can continue working for years making the same mistakes over and over with little insight
- has no obligations whatsoever

Certified Matchmaker Quality Standards

1. All Certified Matchmakers are trained and certified by the Matchmaking Institute and adhere to the highest quality standards in the industry.

2. All Certified Matchmakers follow a strict code of ethics.

3. All Certified Matchmakers are dedicated to a client's right to a personal, supportive, and professional service at all times.

4. All Certified Matchmakers maintain strict confidentiality of all client accounts and will not divulge, discuss, or otherwise exploit any restricted material related to client profile, status, or record of activity.

5. All Certified Matchmakers take the utmost care to deliver the highest standard of service for total customer satisfaction and will be subject to quarterly evaluations correlative of client assessments.

6. All Certified Matchmakers respond to clients' inquiries in a timely fashion and offer complete and clear answers.

7. All Certified Matchmakers are diligent when qualifying all potential matches on behalf of their clients with a personalized approach from beginning to end.

8. All Certified Matchmakers are subject to additional mandatory training and professional development for annual re-certification, in accordance with the Matchmaking Institute's guidelines.

More About the Matchmaking Institute

The Matchmaking Institute, created in 2003 by Jerome Chasques and Lisa Clampitt, CSW, was established to set a code of ethics and strict quality standards in the matchmaking industry. It is the first institute offering matchmaking training and certification, introducing singles to Certified Matchmakers, and providing matchmakers with a network of peers and support.

The mainstream success of online dating has opened the door to using a third party to find love and skyrocketed the popularity of modern-day, one-on-one, personalized matchmaking services. Now more than ever before, it is acceptable to use a matchmaker, but with this growth of the matchmaking market comes a greater need for quality control in the industry. With years of exposure to the pros and cons of the market, our team has collaborated in the creation of a new generation of matchmaking.

www.matchmakinginstitute.com

Matchmaking Institute Founders

Jerome Chasques is a co-founder of the Matchmaking Institute. He also runs a publishing company in New York City and has successfully managed four different businesses over the last fourteen years. He holds a Master's Degree in Business and Finance from Institute d'Etudes Politiques de Paris (Sciences Po) and a Master's Degree in Business Law. The new concept he created in 2002, Dinner in the Dark, has been featured in many publications both nationwide and worldwide. Prior to founding the Matchmaking Institute, Jerome produced educational and cultural programs on CD-ROMs and DVDs in Europe, including the award-winning *The Louvre Museum* title. In 1998, Jerome founded Mr. Cinema, an entertainment news portal, later acquired by Liberty Surf Group, a subsidiary of Bernard Arnault's fashion group LVMH. Jerome loves connecting people and always brings innovative products and concepts on the market. Jerome is married and lives in New York City; he and his wife Nathalie just celebrated their ten year anniversary.

Lisa Clampitt, CSW, is a cofounder and executive director of the Matchmaking Institute, a professional matchmaker and a New York State Certified Social Worker for over fifteen years. She was educated at New York University, receiving a BA in Dramatic Literature, and received her graduate degree, a Masters in Social Work, from the University of Michigan. Lisa has many years of experience in individual and couples counseling as well as relationship and date coaching and has owned her own very successful matchmaking company, VIP Life, for over six years. With this experience and an extensive knowledge of the matchmaking industry under her belt, she went on to create the Matchmaking Institute in order to train and certify others, establishing a strict code of ethics in this important industry. Lisa is consistently sought after as a matchmaking and relationship expert and has had extensive international press coverage. Lisa is married and lives in New York City with her husband Frank.

Thanks

I want to acknowledge someone very special who I was lucky enough to have enter my life at the right time. So here is a very grateful thanks to Sarah B. Parsons for her ongoing support, and for making the creation of this book a true mission from the heart.

Feedback

We value the feedback of our readers very highly. Feel free to send your comments, suggestions, questions, or even testimonials to:

Matchmaking Institute™
89 Fifth Avenue, Suite 602
New York, NY 10003
USA

feedback@matchmakinginstitute.com

Personal Notes

_____

_____

_____

_____

_____

_____

_____

_____

_____

_____

_____